Cambridge Elements ≡

Elements in Comparative Political Theory
edited by
Leigh K. Jenco
London School of Economics

MAIMONIDES AND JEWISH THEOCRACY

The Human Hand of Divine Rule

Charles H. T. Lesch
The Hebrew University of Jerusalem

CAMBRIDGE
UNIVERSITY PRESS

Shaftesbury Road, Cambridge CB2 8EA, United Kingdom

One Liberty Plaza, 20th Floor, New York, NY 10006, USA

477 Williamstown Road, Port Melbourne, VIC 3207, Australia

314–321, 3rd Floor, Plot 3, Splendor Forum, Jasola District Centre,
New Delhi – 110025, India

103 Penang Road, #05–06/07, Visioncrest Commercial, Singapore 238467

Cambridge University Press is part of Cambridge University Press & Assessment,
a department of the University of Cambridge.

We share the University's mission to contribute to society through the pursuit of
education, learning and research at the highest international levels of excellence.

www.cambridge.org
Information on this title: www.cambridge.org/9781108793421

DOI: 10.1017/9781108884051

© Charles H. T. Lesch 2024

This work is in copyright. It is subject to statutory exceptions and to the provisions
of relevant licensing agreements; with the exception of the Creative Commons version
the link for which is provided below, no reproduction of any part of this work may take
place without the written permission of Cambridge University Press.

An online version of this work is published at doi.org/10.1017/9781108884051
under a Creative Commons Open Access license CC-BY-NC-ND 4.0 which permits
re-use, distribution and reproduction in any medium for non-commercial purposes
providing appropriate credit to the original work is given. You may not
distribute derivative works without permission. To view a copy of this licence, visit
https://creativecommons.org/licenses/by-nc-nd/4.0

All versions of this work may contain content reproduced under license from third
parties. Permission to reproduce this third-party content must be obtained from these
third-parties directly.

When citing this work, please include a reference to the DOI 10.1017/9781108884051

First published 2024

A catalogue record for this publication is available from the British Library.

ISBN 978-1-009-46811-4 Hardback
ISBN 978-1-108-79342-1 Paperback
ISSN 2633-3597 (online)
ISSN 2633-3589 (print)

Cambridge University Press & Assessment has no responsibility for the persistence
or accuracy of URLs for external or third-party internet websites referred to in this
publication and does not guarantee that any content on such websites is, or will
remain, accurate or appropriate.

Maimonides and Jewish Theocracy

The Human Hand of Divine Rule

Elements in Comparative Political Theory

DOI: 10.1017/9781108884051
First published online: November 2024

Charles H. T. Lesch
The Hebrew University of Jerusalem

Author for correspondence: Charles H. T. Lesch, charles.lesch@mail.huji.ac.il

Abstract: Theocratic movements are on the rise. But what does it actually mean for God to rule? This study offers one answer by recovering the theocratic project of medieval Judaism's most important thinker, Moses Maimonides. Theocracy is often thought to quash human agency, evoking an overpowering deity and clerical domination. Yet by reconsidering Maimonides' debt to the Islamic philosopher al-Fārābī, and challenging Leo Strauss' influential reading, I argue that among Maimonides' aims was to elevate humanity's role in divine rule. In its highest form, reason is identical with revelation, action with providence. God's governance is delegated: Theocracy requires human agency – the imitation of God. Maimonides focuses on philosophical-religious leaders. But he also broadens *imitatio dei* to anyone whose knowledge of God inspires love of God: By emulating God's goodness, we can become agents of divine rule. In this way, Maimonides' ideas suggest ways by which theocracy and democracy might, counterintuitively, be reconciled. This title is also available as open access on Cambridge Core.

Keywords: Maimonides, Jewish political thought, al-Farabi, democracy, theocracy

© Charles H. T. Lesch 2024

ISBNs: 9781009468114 (HB), 9781108793421 (PB), 9781108884051 (OC)
ISSNs: 2633-3597 (online), 2633-3589 (print)

Contents

Rabbi Yehuda said in the name of Rav: When Moses ascended to the heavens, he found the Holy One, Blessed be He, sitting and attaching crowns to the letters. He said before Him, "Master of the Universe! Who is staying Your hand?" [God] said to him, "There is one man who will exist after many generations, and Akiva ben Yosef is his name, who will in the future expound [li-derosh] on every crown and crown piles and piles of laws."

Babylonian Talmud, Tractate Menachot[1]

It is hard to understand Moses' question, "Who is staying Your hand?" – what is meant by this? . . . God is making the letters into "kings." . . . God will not give any further direction as to the meaning of the laws of the Torah, because its meaning is "not in heaven" [Deuteronomy 30:12].

R. Moshe Feinstein, Igrot Moshe[2]

Let all your deeds be for the sake of heaven.

Pirkei Avot [Ethics of the Fathers][3]

Preface: Theocracy and the Rule of God

This study recovers the theocratic project of medieval Judaism's most important philosopher and jurist, Moses Maimonides. Maimonides himself never uses the term "theocracy." Nor does he anticipate its contemporary social-scientific meaning, traceable to Max Weber, where a predatory clerical elite governs in God's name – a "hierocracy."[4] What Maimonides does do, I will argue, is orient human thought and action around the original theocratic idea: the rule of God. This definition – and the term *theokratia* – was first introduced by the Roman-Jewish historian Josephus, who identified theocracy as Judaism's authentic political theory and described it in Greek philosophical terms.[5] Yet the idea of divine rule predates this Hellenistic formulation. The Hebrew Bible often portrays God as Israel's king. And in the text's prophetic critique of monarchy, purely secular power is framed as

---

[1] Talmud Bavli, Tractate Menachot, 29b.

[2] Moshe Feinstein, *Responsa of Rav Moshe Feinstein*, trans. Moshe David Tendler, Vol. 1 (Hoboken: Ktav, 1996), introduction.

[3] Mishnah, Tractate Pirkei Avot, 2:12.

[4] Weber associates hierocracy with two forms of religious rulership: "(1) a ruler who is legitimated by priests, either as an incarnation or in the name of God, and (2) a high priest is also king." *Economy and Society*, trans. Ephraim Fischoff et al. (Berkeley: University of California Press, [1922] 1978), 1159.

[5] As Carlos Fraenkel has argued, Josephus sought to identify the God of Moses with the God of the Greek philosophers, like Plato and Anaxagoras, who conceived of the divine as *nous*. *Philosophical Religions from Plato to Spinoza* (New York: Cambridge University Press, 2012), 103–04. For valuable background on Judaism's diverse understandings of divine rule and its implications for human rule, see the essays by Moshe Halbertal and Clifford Orwin in the first volume of the *Jewish Political Tradition*. Menachem Lorberbaum, Michael Walzer, and Noam Zohar, ed., *The Jewish Political Tradition, Volume 1: Authority* (New Haven: Yale University Press, 2000). For several approaches to God's rule in modern Jewish thought, see Miguel Vatter, *Living Law: Jewish Political Theology from Hermann Cohen to Hannah Arendt* (New York: Oxford University Press, 2021).

illicit, even idolatrous: "It is Me they have rejected as king," says God, famously, to Samuel.[6] Here and elsewhere in the biblical narrative, the very request for human sovereignty signals spiritual decay. God alone should reign – not only in heaven but on earth.[7]

This definition also gives rise to a paradox. In theory, God's sovereignty eliminates the need for earthly ethics and politics. In practice, something like human agency always remains necessary. The deity, after all, does not punish criminals, collect taxes, defend borders, or feed the hungry; these tasks must be performed by people. But if that is so, what does it actually mean for God to rule? How can we recognize such rulership in practice? And by what means, if any, can it be realized?

My principal aim in this study is to describe how Maimonides answers these questions. By reconstructing the theocratic project implicit in Maimonides' writings, I aim to shed new light on Jewish political thought and medieval political philosophy, as well as contribute to current debates about theocracy's meaning and implications. At the same time, my ancillary aim is to suggest that Maimonides' response to the theocratic paradox offers resources for thinking about theocracy today. This is a work of comparative political theory; while interpretive and historical in method, it also seeds a normative ground. Maimonides' complex account of divine rule – and humanity's role in effecting it – has the potential to, if not resolve, then at least complicate the common portrait of theocracy and democracy as irreconcilable foes.

Introduction: The Return of Theocracy and Maimonides' Politics Reconsidered

"In a liberal democracy," writes Jürgen Habermas, "state power has lost its religious aura . . . It is hard to see on which normative grounds the historical step toward the secularization of state power could ever be reversed."[8] Habermas' words reflect a more general thesis: A core feature of modernity is the uncoupling of political legitimacy from religious authority.[9] One aspect of this thesis is sociological. By this view, the secularization of politics should be couched in larger historical

---

[6] 1 Samuel, 8:7.

[7] See for example José Faur, *The Horizontal Society: Understanding the Covenant and Alphabetic Judaism*, 2 Vols. (Boston: Academic Studies Press, 2009), 1.127. For an example of how God's exclusive sovereignty was invoked in modern political theory, see my "Theopolitics Contra Political Theology: Martin Buber's Biblical Critique of Carl Schmitt," *American Political Science Review* 113, no. 1 (2019).

[8] Jürgen Habermas, "'The Political': The Rational Meaning of a Questionable Inheritance of Political Theology," in *The Power of Religion in the Public Sphere*, ed. Eduardo Mendieta and Jonathan VanAntwerpen (New York: Columbia University Press, 2011), 24.

[9] For prominent expressions of this thesis, see John Rawls, "The Idea of Public Reason Revisited," *The University of Chicago Law Review* 64, no. 3 (1997); Charles Taylor, *A Secular Age* (Cambridge: Belknap of Harvard University Press, 2007).

shifts – in the collapse of a unified cosmos or the "disenchantment of the world."[10] Yet as historians of political thought have long known, secularization was not only a sociological process but a normative project.[11] The creation of an autonomous political sphere, one liberated from theology and governed by its own *raison d'état*, was an aim shared by thinkers as diverse as Hobbes and Locke, Sieyès and Constant, Marx and Mill, Rawls and Nozick. And as Habermas' words show, this trend continues. Theocracy has been marked for extinction. With rare exceptions, political theory, like politics itself, no longer grounds its claims in God.

God, however, is increasingly on the march. Over the past several years, movements with theocratic aspirations have gained in both intellectual influence and real power throughout the world. In 2014, ISIS declared itself an Islamic "caliphate," and at one point controlled broad swaths of territory in Iraq and Syria. In Israel, a political party openly calling for replacing democracy with religious rule sits in the present governing coalition. And in the United States, the rise of Christian nationalism has brought dominion theology and Catholic integralism into the political mainstream. Such punctures in the secularization thesis have prompted a range of scholarly responses. Political scientists have produced a rich empirical literature on religion and democratic citizenship.[12] Sociologists have investigated the phenomenology of "post-secularism" and "desecularization."[13] And political theorists, often building on Carl Schmitt's theory of "political theology," have uncovered theological sources behind modernity, human rights, liberalism, democracy, and solidarity.[14]

---

[10] Peter Berger, *The Sacred Canopy* (Garden City: Anchor Books, 1969); Marcel Gauchet, *The Disenchantment of the World: A Political History of Religion*, trans. Oscar Burge (Princeton: Princeton University Press, [1985] 1997); Max Weber, "Science as a Vocation," in *From Max Weber: Essays in Sociology*, ed. H. H. Gerth and C. Wright Mills (New York: Oxford University Press, [1917] 1958).

[11] Hans Blumenberg, *The Legitimacy of the Modern Age*, trans. Robert M. Wallace (Cambridge, MA: MIT Press, [1966] 1983); Julie Cooper, *Secular Powers: Humility in Modern Political Thought* (Chicago: The University of Chicago Press, 2013); Michel Foucault, *Security, Territory, Population*, ed. Michel Senellart, trans. Graham Burchell (New York: Picador, 1978); Karl Löwith, *Meaning in History: The Theological Implications of the Philosophy of History* (Chicago: The University of Chicago Press, [1949] 1957); Steven B. Smith, *Modernity and Its Discontents* (New Haven: Yale University Press, 2018).

[12] See for instance Gizem Arikan and Pazit Ben-Nun Bloom, "Democratic Norms and Religion," in *The Oxford Encyclopedia of Politics and Religion*, ed. Mark J. Rozell, Paul A. Djupe, and Ted G. Jelen (New York: Oxford University Press, 2020); Robert D. Putnam, *American Grace: How Religion Divides and Unites Us* (New York: Simon & Schuster, 2010).

[13] Talal Asad, *Formations of the Secular: Christianity, Islam, Modernity* (Stanford: Stanford University Press, 2003); Peter Berger, ed., *The Desecularization of the World: Resurgent Religion and World Politics* (Grand Rapids: William B. Eerdmans, 1999); Craig Calhoun, Mark Juergensmeyer, and Jonathan VanAntwerpen, ed. *Rethinking Secularism* (New York: Oxford University Press, 2011); José Casanova, *Public Religions in the Modern World* (Chicago: The University of Chicago Press, 1994).

[14] Carl Schmitt, *Political Theology: Four Chapters on the Concept of Sovereignty*, trans. George Schwab (Chicago: The University of Chicago Press, [1934] 2005). For modernity, see Michael Allen Gillespie, *The Theological Origins of Modernity* (Chicago: The University of

Yet an important theoretical lacuna remains: the normative and conceptual analysis of theocracy itself.[15] One might be tempted to dismiss theocracy's rise as a political-psychological aberration – an outgrowth of contemporary anomie, fracture, and conspiratorial thinking. But theocracy is also a political theory; it makes fundamental claims about justice, morality, and authority; and it has a long and complex intellectual history. Thus if theocracy truly is emerging as a rival to liberal democracy, Habermas' confident assertions should be reposed as questions: In age in which political legitimacy is understood in almost universally secular terms, why do theocratic ideas retain their appeal? Are there, in fact, "normative grounds" for desecularizing governance? What, in short, has theocracy meant, and what might it still mean today?

In this study, I contribute a new perspective to these questions by elucidating Maimonides' theocratic project. Maimonides has been the subject of a vast scholarly literature, including first-rate studies of his political thought in general, and on specific issues such as kingship, required beliefs, social ethics, messianism, and the philosophy of law.[16] He is a central figure not only in

---

Chicago Press, 2008). For human rights, see Samuel Moyn, *Christian Human Rights* (Philadelphia: University of Pennsylvania Press, 2015). For liberalism, see Eric Nelson, *The Theology of Liberalism* (Cambridge, MA: Harvard University Press, 2019). For democracy, see Miguel Vatter, *Divine Democracy: Political Theology after Carl Schmitt* (New York: Oxford University Press, 2021). For solidarity, see my *Solidarity in a Secular Age: From Political Theology to Jewish Philosophy* (New York: Oxford University Press, 2022).

[15] There have been notable exceptions to this neglect of theocracy, especially in recent years. On Jewish theocracy in particular, see Alexander Kaye, *The Invention of Jewish Theocracy: The Struggle for Legal Authority in Modern Israel* (New York: Oxford University Press, 2020); Benjamin Pollock, "'Every State Becomes a Theocracy': Hermann Cohen on the Israelites under Divine Rule," *Jewish Studies Quarterly* 25, no. 2 (2018); Vatter, *Living Law: Jewish Political Theology from Hermann Cohen to Hannah Arendt*. A recent volume which offers a variety of perspectives on the concept, *Challenging Theocracy*, also includes an essay by Alan Mittleman on theocratic ideas in Judaism, though his treatment of Maimonides, in contrast to mine, centers around political institutions like the monarchy. "Theocratic Arguments in Judaism," in *Challenging Theocracy: Ancient Lessons for Global Politics*, ed. Toivo Koivukoski, David Edward Tabachnick, and Hermínio Meireles Teixeira (Toronto: University of Toronto Press, 2018). On juridical instantiations of theocracy, see Ran Hirschl, *Constitutional Theocracy* (Cambridge, MA: Harvard University Press, 2010).

[16] Gerald Blidstein, *'Ekronot mediniyim be-mishnat ha-Rambam [Political concepts in Maimonidean jurisprudence]* (Ramat-Gan: Bar-Ilan, 1983); Amos Funkenstein, *Nature, History, and Messianism in Maimonides [Hebrew]* (Tel Aviv: Misrad Ha-Bitachon, 1983); Lenn E. Goodman, "Maimonides' Philosophy of Law," *Jewish Law Annual* 1 (1978); W. Zev Harvey, "Bein filosofiyah medinit le-halakhah be-mishnat ha-Rambam [Between Political Philosophy and Halakhah in Maimonides' Teachings]," *Iyyun* 29 (1980); Menachem Kellner, *Dogma in Medieval Jewish Thought* (New York: Oxford University Press, 2004); Howard Kreisel, *Maimonides' Political Thought: Studies in Ethics, Law, and the Human Ideal* (Albany: SUNY Press, 1999); Menachem Lorberbaum, *Politics and the Limits of Law: Secularizing the Political in Medieval Jewish Thought* (Stanford: Stanford University Press, 2002); Abraham Melamed, *Wisdom's Little Sister: Studies in Medieval and Renaissance Jewish Political Thought* (Boston: Academic Studies Press, 2012). Comprehensive treatments of Maimonides' life and thought include Herbert Alan Davidson, *Moses Maimonides*

Jewish studies but in philosophy, where his influence on a diverse range of thinkers – in the West and in Islam, from the Middle Ages through the present – has been well-documented.[17] Even so, he has only rarely been interpreted as theorist of theocracy.[18] And with few and notable exceptions (which I address below), he is not frequently read by political theorists.[19] This oversight is understandable: While there are political arguments throughout Maimonides' corpus, his philosophical masterpiece, *The Guide to the Perplexed*, is framed as addressing not rule and collective governance, but theological puzzles (how can we know a transcendent God, the existence of evil) and individual tensions (philosophy and Judaism, contemplation and action). His legal writings, including his monumental *Mishneh Torah [Code of Law, lit. "Repetition of the Torah"]*, encompass the whole range of Jewish law and belief, much of it having no connection to politics. His ethical texts are concerned with cultivating virtue. He left us no explicit work of political theory.

Yet by revisiting Maimonides' debt to the Islamic philosopher al-Fārābī, I argue that among Maimonides' core aims was to transform the meaning of God's rule – and, especially, humanity's role in realizing it. Theocracy is often

---

(Oxford: Oxford University Press, 2005); Moshe Halbertal, *Maimonides: Life and Thought*, trans. Joel Linsider (Princeton: Princeton University Press, [2009] 2014); Joel L. Kraemer, *Maimonides: The Life and World of One of Civilization's Greatest Minds* (New York: Doubleday Religious Publishing Group, 2008); Aviezer Ravitzky, *Maimonides: Traditionalism, Originality, and Revolution* (Jerusalem: Merkaz Shazar Press, 2009); Kenneth Seeskin, ed., *The Cambridge Companion to Maimonides* (Cambridge: Cambridge University Press, 2005); Sarah Stroumsa, *Maimonides in His World: Portrait of a Mediterranean Thinker* (Princeton: Princeton University Press, 2009).

[17] Jay Harris, ed., *Maimonides after 800 Years: Essays on Maimonides and His Influence* (Cambridge, MA: Harvard University Press, 2007); Carlos Fraenkel, ed., *Traditions of Maimonideanism* (Boston: Brill, 2009); Menachem Kellner, *Reinventing Maimonides in Contemporary Jewish Thought* (New York: Oxford University Press, 2021); Kenneth Seeskin, *Searching for a Distant God* (New York: Oxford University Press, 2000); Mark Shapiro, *Studies in Maimonides and His Interpreters* (Scranton: University of Scranton Press, 2008); Joseph Stern, *Problems and Parables of Law: Maimonides and Nahmanides on Reasons for the Commandments (ta'amei ha-mitzvot)* (New York: State University of New York Press, 1988); Georges Tamer, ed., *The Trias of Maimonides* (New York: Walter de Gruyter, 2005).

[18] For exceptions, see Ella Belfer, *Am Yisrael u-Malkhut Shamayim [The People of Israel and the Kingdom of Heaven]* (Ramat-Gan: Bar-Ilan, 1980); Aviezer Ravitzky, *Religion and State in Jewish Philosophy: Models of Unity, Division, and Subordination* (Jerusalem: Israel Democracy Institute, 2002); Gershon Weiler, *Jewish Theocracy* (Leiden: Brill, [1976] 1988). As with Alan Mittleman's aforementioned essay, each of these texts consider Maimonides as a theocratic thinker largely with reference to his juridical and institutional ideas, rather than his more basic philosophical and theological approach.

[19] In addition to Leo Strauss, who I discuss further on, his student Ralph Lerner has written widely on Maimonides. Leo Strauss, *Philosophy and Law: Contributions to the Understanding of Maimonides and His Predecessors*, trans. Eve Adler (Albany: SUNY Press, [1935] 1995); Ralph Lerner, *Maimonides' Empire of Light: Popular Enlightenment in an Age of Belief* (Chicago: University of Chicago Press, 2000). See also Joshua Parens, *Maimonides and Spinoza: Their Conflicting Views of Human Nature* (Chicago: University of Chicago Press, 2012).

thought to quash human agency: It evokes an overpowering God and Weber's repressive clerics (or Dostoevsky's Grand Inquisitor). Likewise in Maimonides' own time, many thinkers, including Jewish ones, sought to zealously guard God's omnipotence – minimizing human freedom, insulating revelation from reason, and making God the author of every natural cause and individual choice. For Maimonides, by contrast, individual providence is up to us. Gifted with free will, we can discipline ourselves, cultivate our virtue, and, through the careful study of the sciences and philosophy, attain theoretical knowledge of God. And when we succeed, we come not only to know and love God; we serve as agents of divine rule on earth, acting on insights gleaned from accessing the Active Intellect, the lowest level in Maimonides' Neoplatonic cosmology. In its highest form, therefore, human reason is identical with revelation, human action with providence. Maimonides, to be sure, thought this achievement was rare. But just as the intellect has gradations, from true belief to real knowledge, so too does providence. Divine rule is delegated: Theocracy – the governance of God – *requires*, rather than reduces, human agency. Whether God rules is in our hands.

To be clear, my aim here is not a wholesale revision of Maimonides. To advance my thesis, I sometimes take sides in interpretative disagreements without being able to fully argue for my position (though I do try to cite these disputes where possible). And perhaps the best-known of these debates – about whether and how Maimonides' *Guide* should be read esoterically – originates from his most famous reader in political theory, a thinker who likewise regarded Maimonides' project (or "teaching") as both indebted to al-Fārābī and deeply, though covertly, political: Leo Strauss.

Strauss first argued that the *Guide* has a secret message in two essays which appeared within a year of one another in the mid-1930s.[20] Both are premised on a basic assumption: the unbridgeable gap between law and philosophy, revelation and reason, Jerusalem and Athens. Maimonides, according to Strauss, regarded philosophy as alien to the Torah. He "took it for granted that being a Jew and being a philosopher are mutually exclusive."[21] Consequently, the *Guide*, for Strauss, cannot be about its overt aims – philosophy, theology, ethics, or even religion. Its true aims instead are "political," based on a "necessary

---

[20] The first essay was originally delivered by Strauss at a 1935 conference at Columbia University, contemporaneous with the appearance of his book-length study of Maimonides, *Philosophy and Law*. The essay was published again in 1941, and reprinted in *Persecution and the Art of Writing* as "The Literary Character of the *Guide for the Perplexed*." *Persecution and the Art of Writing* (Chicago: University of Chicago Press, 1952). The second essay appeared as a 1936 article, "Quelques Remarques sur la Science Politique de Maïmonide et de Farabi" in *Revue des Etudes Juives*. My citations here are from Robert Bartlett's translation "Some Remarks on the Political Science of Maimonides and Farabi," *Interpretation* 18, no. 1 ([1936] 1990).

[21] Strauss, *Persecution*, 19.

connection between politics and metaphysics (theology)," rooted in Plato, and transmitted via the "Platonizing politics of al-Fārābī."[22] What is the nature of this politics? According to Strauss, the metaphysical discussions we find in Plato's *Laws*, al-Fārābī's *The Political Regime*, and Maimonides' *Guide* are merely rhetoric designed to sustain social order for the sake of a philosophical elite. Indeed cultivating obedience, according to Strauss (and following Spinoza), was the Torah's chief aim too: "the teaching of these philosophical disciplines ... is identical with the secret teaching of the Bible."[23] "Law" is imposed on the vulgar; "philosophy" is practiced by the wise. The two groups should be kept separate. And Maimonides, perceiving an unbridgeable gap between the active and contemplative life, sought to secure, via the *Guide*, a situation where the latter could persist.[24]

Fully addressing Strauss' thesis would require tracing it back through his analyses of medieval Islamic thought and Plato, something beyond the scope of this study.[25] Moreover, one of the characteristics of esoteric reading is that it cannot be disproven: Any data point one might cite against it can be reinterpreted as further evidence in its favor – evidence, in Herbert Davidson's words, for "how deep the plot ran."[26] My aim vis-à-vis Strauss will thus be a more modest one: to show that a theocratic reading of the *Guide* is just as viable as one based on "Platonic politics."[27] Strauss, I believe, was importantly right about both the political nature of Maimonides' project and his debt to al-Fārābī. Where he erred was in interpreting that project as a secret critique of Judaism and his reading of al-Fārābī as esoteric. Whatever al-Fārābī's own intentions, Maimonides, I will argue, took his predecessor's thought as providing a serious metaphysical and political roadmap for manifesting divine rule. And he saw in the center of that map not a route toward contemplative withdrawal, but one

---

[22] Strauss, *Philosophy and Law*, 58; "Remarks," 6.   [23] *Persecution*, 45–46.

[24] "Remarks," 20.

[25] For a comprehensive critique of Strauss' approach, see Lenn E. Goodman, *A Guide to the* Guide to the Perplexed: *A Reader's Companion to Maimonides' Masterwork* (Stanford: Stanford University Press, 2024). For Strauss and medieval Islamic thought, see Rasoul Namazi, *Leo Strauss and Islamic Political Thought* (New York: Cambridge University Press, 2022); Joshua Parens, *Leo Strauss and the Recovery of Medieval Political Philosophy* (Rochester: University of Rochester Press, 2016). For more on esoteric writing, see Arthur M. Melzer, *Philosophy between the Lines: The Lost History of Esoteric Writing* (Chicago: University of Chicago Press, 2014).

[26] Herbert Alan Davidson, *Moses Maimonides*, 400. A further mark against Strauss' thesis: Maimonides did not hold back in documenting the humiliating experience of Jews living as *dhimmis* under Islamic rule. Goodman, *A Guide to the* Guide to the Perplexed, Part III. Moreoever, as Sarah Stroumsa has shown, Andalusian Aristotelians – Jewish and Muslim – were rarely targeted for persecution. *Andalus and Sefarad: On Philosophy and Its History in Islamic Spain* (Princeton: Princeton University Press, 2019), 95.

[27] Moshe Halbertal offers a valuable typology of different major approaches to the *Guide* which have been taken historically. *Maimonides*, 277–362.

where true knowledge, identified with revelation, manifests in moral and political action. Maimonides does distinguish between the philosophical elite and ordinary people. He was not an Enlightenment thinker and did not write in such a context. But neither does he try to dupe the masses into serving the privileged. He seeks to bring both, according to their abilities, to true ideas about God.

I begin by examining the role of al-Fārābī's "first ruler," a philosopher-prophet-legislator who, by imitating divine governance, acts as God's viceroy on earth. Maimonides, I show through a close reading of the introduction to his youthful *Commentary on the Mishnah*, applies al-Fārābī's template to Israel's rabbinic leaders and legal texts. He then applies it again in the *Guide* to Moses and the Torah itself. While God exercises a general providence through the natural cycles of form and matter, he delegates individual providence to us. God's rule on earth, in other words, requires *human* rule – an imitation of God. Yet while al-Fārābī, an eternalist, models his *imitatio dei* on Plato's *Timaeus*, I argue that Maimonides, who in the *Guide* incorporates important elements of theological voluntarism, draws on his own concept of God. In doing so he broadens the scope of divine rule: Maimonides makes it the task not only of a sui generis "first ruler", but of anyone whose knowledge of God motivates his love of God. A critical but concealed aim of the *Guide* is thus to identify, train, and motivate such individuals. And this finding, already unorthodox, suggests an even more striking implication: Maimonides' project was not only to *describe* God's rule; it was to *realize* it. Maimonides' ideas, I conclude, suggest innovative ways by which theocracy and democracy might, counterintuitively, be reconciled.

1 "God's Governance in Another Way": Delegating Divine Rule in Al-Fārābī

Maimonides' debt to al-Fārābī has been known since at least Salomon Munk's nineteenth-century French translation of the *Guide*, and following the appearance of Strauss' essays, scholars have tracked it across a range of Maimonidean themes and texts.[28] Strauss pinned it to al-Fārābī's *The Principles of Beings* – a work

---

[28] Scholars have long recognized Maimonides' debt to al-Fārābī on such questions as epistemology, prophecy, virtue, belief, and relationship between philosophy, religion, and law more generally. See for example Lawrence V. Berman, "Maimonides, the Disciple of Alfarabi," *Israel Oriental Studies* 4 (1974); Alfred Ivry, "Islamic and Greek Influence on Maimonides' Philosophy," in *Maimonides and Philosophy*, ed. Shlomo Pines and Yirmiyahu Yovel (Dordrecht: Martinus Nijhoff, 1986); Joel L. Kraemer, "Alfarabi's Opinions of the Virtuous City and Maimonides' Foundations of the Law," in *Studia Orientalia Memoriae D. H. Baneth Dedicata* (Jerusalem: Magnes Press, 1979); Jeffrey Macy, "A Study in Medieval Jewish and Arabic Political Philosophy: Maimonides' Shemonah Peraqim and Al-Farabi's Fusul Al-Madani (or Fusul Muntaza'ah)" (PhD. The Hebrew University of Jerusalem, 1982); Shlomo Pines, "The Philosophical Sources of the Guide of the Perplexed," in *The Guide of the Perplexed* (Chicago: University of Chicago Press, 1963); Shlomo Pines, "The Limitations of Human Knowledge

which, as Strauss noted, bears the "authentic title" *The Political Regime*, and which Maimonides, in a famous letter to his translator, singled out by name: "All that al-Fārābī wrote, and in particular the *Treatise on the Principles of Beings*, is entirely without fault . . . for he excelled in wisdom."[29] Here I will argue for the equally formative effect of a different Farabian text: his *Book of Religion*. While Maimonides drew from across al-Fārābī's oeuvre, *Religion* is distinctive in describing how human rule, properly constituted, can serve as an extension of divine rule. God, for al-Fārābī, governs on earth through human beings. In this way, he gives Maimonides the language to frame and articulate his theocratic aims.

Toward the end of *Religion*, al-Fārābī discusses the purpose and methods of "political science," a discipline focused on different ranks of human and divine "rulership." He concludes by linking the two together:

> [Political science] explains how revelation descends from Him level by level until it reaches the first ruler who thus governs the city or the nation and nations with what revelation from God brings. . . . It explains this in that God is also the governor of the virtuous city, just as He is the governor of the world, and in that His governance of the world takes place in one way, whereas His governance of the virtuous city takes place in another way; there is, however, a relation between the two kinds of governing.[30]

Al-Fārābī is a complex and enigmatic thinker, and the full meaning of this passage is not easy to discern at first blush.[31] My first task is thus to elucidate it – to explain al-Fārābī's terms, and, in particular, to make sense of what he means

---

According to al-Farabi, Ibn Bajja, and Maimonides," in *Studies in Medieval Jewish History and Literature*, ed. Isadore Twersky (Cambridge, MA: Harvard University Press, 1979). As much of this literature was inspired by Strauss, however, my argument naturally departs from it in important respects. For alternative views, see Herbert Alan Davidson, "Maimonides' Shemonah Peraqim and Alfarabi's Fusul al-Madani," *Proceedings of the American Academy of Jewish Research* 31 (1963); Fraenkel, *Philosophical Religions*; Abraham Melamed, *The Philosopher-King in Medieval and Renaissance Jewish Political Thought* (Albany: State University of New York Press, 2003).

[29] "Remarks," 6. See Moses Maimonides, *Letters of Maimonides*, ed. Isaac Shailat (Jerusalem: Maaliyot Press, 1988), 553. While Averroes also comes in for praise in this letter – something to which Pines, in his *Guide* introduction, calls special attention – scholars now believe that his name was a later interpolation by a Jewish Averroist, further highlighting al-Fārābī's centrality. Doron Forte, "Back to the Sources: Alternative Versions of Maimonides' Letter to Samuel Ibn Tibbon and their Neglected Significance," *Jewish Studies Quarterly* 23 (2016).

[30] al-Farabi, "Book of Religion," in *The Political Writings: "Selected Aphorisms" and Other Texts* (Ithaca: Cornell University Press, 2015), 112.

[31] My reading of al-Fārābī focuses on those aspects germane to Maimonides and theocracy. For more general treatments of his political thought which accord, in varying degrees, with Strauss' position, see Charles E. Butterworth, "Alfarabi's Goal: Political Philosophy, not Political Theology," in *Islam, the State, and Political Authority: Medieval Issues and Modern Concerns*, ed. Asma Afsaruddin (New York: Palgrave-MacMillan, 2011); Miriam Galston, *Politics and Excellence: The Political Philosophy of Alfarabi* (Princeton: Princeton University

in saying that God governs the virtuous city "in another way." How al-Fārābī defined these terms was, we will see, also critical for Maimonides' own understanding of divine rule: emanation, revelation, providence, happiness, and especially, the "first ruler" and religion.[32]

For al-Fārābī, as for many medieval thinkers, not only were "metaphysics" and "theology" bound together as a single discipline; both were infused with a political dimension: To study God's providence was to study His "rule" or "Lordship."[33] The means of such rule, above all, was "emanation." In Neoplatonic philosophy – originating in figures like Plotinus and Proclus and then adopted, via the Graeco-Arabic translation movement, by many Islamic philosophers and by Maimonides – emanation explains how the world can exist independently of God while remaining tethered, in some sense, to the divine.[34] Unlike an occasionalist model in which God materially controls (indeed recreates) every atom at every moment, emanation stresses the deity's role not in matter but form. Through the unfolding of ideas, God bestows reality on all creatures. He sustains their essence: Given that matter

---

Press, 1990); Muhsin S. Mahdi, *Alfarabi and the Foundation of Islamic Political Philosophy* (Chicago: University of Chicago Press, 2001); Alexander Orwin, *Redefining the Muslim Community: Ethnicity, Religion, and Politics in the Thought of Alfarabi* (Philadelphia: University of Pennsylvania Press, 2017); Joshua Parens, *An Islamic Philosophy of Virtuous Religions: Introducing Alfarabi* (Albany: SUNY Press, 2006). For a critique of the Straussian approach, see Dimitri Gutas, "The Study of Arabic Philosophy in the Twentieth Century," *British Journal of Middle Eastern Studies* 29 (2002). For a comprehensive study of al-Fārābī from an alternative perspective, see Philippe Vallat, *Farabi et l'École d'Alexandrie* (Paris: Vrin, 2004).

[32] My claim is not that Maimonides' way of understanding these ideas derived exclusively from al-Fārābī. As scholars have long documented, Maimonides was familiar with and drew inspiration from a host of philosophers, both ancient (Plato, Aristotle, Galen, Plotinus, Alexander, Proclus) and what he called "modern" (al-Fārābī, Avicenna, Ibn Bājjah, Ibn Tufayl, Averroes), including those he criticized (al-Ghazali). My argument instead is that tracing al-Fārābī's influence helps to illuminate Maimonides' theocratic aims in particular. For a rich treatment of Maimonides' intellectual context, see Stroumsa, *Maimonides in His World*.

[33] As evidence that the *Guide* "cannot be called a theological work," Strauss argues that "Maimonides does not know theology as a discipline distinct from metaphysics." *Persecution*, 46. But the same could be said of Aristotle: It was only after Aristotle's death, when his writings were edited, that the term "metaphysics" was applied to what he himself called First Philosophy or theology. See Giovanni Reale, *The Concept of First Philosophy and the Unity of the Metaphysics of Aristotle*, trans. John R. Catan (Albany: SUNY Press, 1980). Thus when Maimonides uses the term "divine science" in referring to the *Ma'aseh Merkavah* – what he identifies as the rabbinic shibboleth for metaphysics – he is plainly talking about theology. The same equation of metaphysics and theology can be found in *Theology of Aristotle*, a pseudo-Aristotelian text, translated into Arabic, which exercised a deep influence on classical Islamic philosophy: "The first chapter of the book of Aristotle the philosopher, called in Greek 'Theologia', that is, discourse on Divine Lordship" (*wa-huwa al-qawl fi l-rububiyya*). An English translation of the text, as well as an illuminating analysis of its meaning and significance, can be found in Peter Adamson's *The Arabic Plotinus* (London: Duckworth, 2002).

[34] For more on the Graeco-Arabic translation movement, see Gutas, "The Study of Arabic Philosophy in the Twentieth Century." For the development of Neoplatonic metaphysics and theology, see Lloyd Gerson, *From Plato to Platonism* (Ithaca: Cornell University Press, 2013).

cannot exist on its own, a thing without form would cease to be. For an emanationist, therefore, what defines things are *ideas*. And human beings, consequently, retain a path to knowing both the world and the divine. When we cognize something's form we call this insight – a fulfilled or actualized mind. And when we develop our insight sufficiently, through knowledge of physics, metaphysics, and theology, we attain the "Active Intellect." This is the lowest rank in the heavenly hierarchy. But it is nonetheless connected, through emanation, to God (the "First Cause").[35]

Emanation allows al-Fārābī to divide divine rule between general and particular providence, and, in this way, to open an important space for human agency. God's providence over the order of nature, via emanation to the supernal intellects and spheres, is ineluctable. Over human beings, however, divine rule is not guaranteed.[36] The ethereal intellects always choose the good. Human beings err: We may not know how we should act; or we may choose, based on our free will, to act in the wrong way. Bad actions arise when we prioritize "the pleasant and the useful, honor, and similar things." Good ones arise when we instead prioritize something al-Fārābī calls "happiness." When we make happiness our ultimate end, he writes, "everything a human being generates is good."[37]

If happiness is the linchpin of divine rule, how can we attain it? Here Neoplatonism's revision of Aristotle becomes crucial. Aristotelian cosmology is sometimes portrayed as abandoning human beings to their fate; the First Cause, thinking only the most perfect thoughts (and therefore only about itself), is utterly

---

[35] al-Farabi, "Political Regime," in *The Political Writings: "Political Regime" and "Summary of Plato's Laws"* (Ithaca: Cornell University Press, 2015), 42–43. For more on the meaning and centrality of emanationist ideas in Maimonides' Arabic philosophical milieu, see Goodman, *A Guide to the* Guide to the Perplexed, Part II. In brief, an important source of Neoplatonic thought was Plato's *Timaeus*, which was widely known in Arabic because of Galen's summary. Because God (or Plato's Demiurge or "Craftsman") was understood to harbor no envy, he exhibited a kind of principle of plenitude, permitting others to participate in reality and develop themselves according to their potential. From Aristotle, Neoplatonists were especially influenced by the idea that nothing in the world is ontologically self-contained, but must instead rely, for its reality, on something beyond itself. This crucially includes the human mind: The mind is unable to will itself to think; it can only do so by virtue of the Active Intellect, in the same way that objects in the world are only illuminated because of the sun's rays. The key to developing in thought, therefore, is to properly attune oneself to its intellectual "light." A critical innovation of Neoplatonists was to see the Active Intellect as not only providing all worldly things with form but also permitting human minds to connect their own powers of reason to the objective rationality of things in the world. In Plotinus' metaphor, for instance, God ("the One") is akin to a candle which can light another candle without losing any of its own light. Crucially, however, divine influence on the world is intellectual, not physical, a point emphasized for example by Alexander of Aphrodisias in his widely-known *On the Cosmos*.

[36] Al-Farabi, "Selected Aphorisms," in *The Political Writings: Selected Aphorisms' and Other Texts*, 56–57.

[37] al-Farabi, *Political Regime*, 64.

unconcerned with the "sublunary" realm – that is, with people.[38] Emanation transforms this dynamic. For by virtue of our contact with the Active Intellect, we retain a link to the deity. And this leads to a radical implication: In its most highly developed form, our mind approaches unity with the divine mind.[39] It is this experience of fully actualizing the intellect – of fusing one's mind with the Active Intellect – that al-Fārābī refers to as "happiness": "When the human intellect achieves its ultimate perfection, its substance comes close to being the substance of this [divine] intellect."[40] Attaining happiness is thus an essentially cognitive endeavor: It requires knowledge of the "superior science" of metaphysics. Indeed al-Fārābī emphasizes that all other intellectual pursuits and individual virtues – including moral virtue – have value only in so far as they contribute toward this end: "These sciences merely follow the example of that [metaphysical] science, which is supreme happiness."[41]

At the same time, al-Fārābī argues that happiness translates not only to the highest form of theoretical insight but also practical knowledge. It tells us how to act. And this is critical, because human social organization often impedes human perfection. Al-Fārābī's question is how these barriers might be dismantled – how the achievement of happiness by one remarkable individual might propagate happiness more broadly. He finds his answer by transposing his ideas into a religious register:

> This human being . . . is the one of whom it ought to be said that he receives revelation. . . . That is, when there remains no intermediary between him and the Active Intellect. . . . Because the Active Intellect is an emanation from the existence of the first cause, it is possible due to this to say that the first cause is what brings revelation to this human being by the intermediary of the Active Intellect.[42]

In philosophy, writes al-Fārābī, the source of happiness is the Active Intellect; in religion, we call it the "holy spirit" or "trustworthy spirit."[43] In philosophy, the Active Intellect bestows theoretical knowledge via the flow of ideas emanating from the first cause; in religion, we call such a flow "revelation." And this leads to a final, remarkable, conclusion. While philosophy would term one who achieves the Active Intellect a "perfect philosopher," in religion, he goes by another name: the "supreme" or "first" ruler.[44]

---

[38] Robert Sharples, "Alexander of Aphrodisias on Divine Providence," *Classical Quarterly* 32 (1982).

[39] Adamson, *The Arabic Plotinus*.

[40] "The Philosophy of Aristotle," trans. Muhsin Mahdi in *Alfarabi's Philosophy of Plato and Aristotle* (New York: The Free Press of Glencoe, 1962), 127.

[41] "The Attainment of Happiness," in *Medieval Political Philosophy: A Sourcebook*, ed. Ralph Lerner and Muhsin Mahdi (New York: Free Press of Glencoe, 1963), 75–76.

[42] *Political Regime*, 69.   [43] *Political Regime*, 30.   [44] *Religion*, 93; *Political Regime*, 69.

2 "The Philosopher, Supreme Ruler, Prince, Legislator, and Imam Is but a Single Idea": Al-Fārābī's "First Ruler"

As many have observed, the first ruler is al-Fārābī's version of Plato's "philosopher king": an individual who, having experienced the truth, is tasked with returning to the cave in order to enlighten his people – to bring them to "happiness."[45] Indeed for al-Fārābī, only by having a capacity for rule can one be a philosopher in the fullest sense: "To be a truly perfect philosopher one has to possess both the theoretical sciences and the faculty for exploiting them for the benefit of all others according to their capacity. Were one to consider the case of the true philosopher, he would find no difference between him and the supreme ruler."[46] Importantly, this means that while a first ruler will be a founding figure, the qualifier "first" marks his intellectual-political rank rather than temporal position. One first ruler might closely follow another, or arise generations later, or never appear again.[47] What distinguishes him is philosophy: the extent to which he has fully actualized his intellect.[48] Thus when al-Fārābī argues, in the passage quoted earlier, that the first ruler is responsible for realizing God's governance on earth, it is the "truly perfect philosopher" who he has in mind. Or as he puts it elsewhere, "the Philosopher, Supreme Ruler, Prince, Legislator, and Imam is but a single idea."[49]

In effecting popular happiness, however, the philosopher hits a number of obstacles. One is circumstantial: resistance from his own society. By himself, a person may have all it takes to transform his philosophy into rulership. Yet "if after reaching this stage no use is made of him" – if his insights are shunned – he will simply retreat into a contemplative life.[50] Three other obstacles are more pervasive. First, for people to grow in knowledge, their society must unify its norms, practices, and institutions around this end. How can such a harmony be achieved? Second, philosophy's insights are universal; yet every group of people is inexorably particular, differing from one another in time, place, and history. By what means can theoretical claims be fit to national forms? Finally, there are wide variations in human reason between different people: In some, it is as robust as can be; in others, it is fledgling and frail. Is it possible to translate complex ideas from physics, metaphysics, and theology into a medium accessible to all? Al-Fārābī's response to each of these questions is the same: the development and dissemination of religion – or, as he calls it in *Religion*, the "kingly craft."[51]

---

[45] See for example Melamed, *Philosopher-King*; Galston, *Politics and Excellence*.

[46] *Attainment of Happiness*, 76.   [47] *Religion*, 99.   [48] *Attainment of Happiness*, 75.

[49] *Attainment of Happiness*, 79.

[50] *Attainment of Happiness*, 81. See also al-Farabi, "The Philosophy of Plato," in *Alfarabi's Philosophy of Plato and Aristotle* (New York: Free Press of Glencoe, 1962), 62–63.

[51] *Religion*, 97–107.

For al-Fārābī, the kingly craft is the means by which a nation's first ruler directs his people toward ultimate happiness and divine rule. He describes it as a kind of imitation of God applied to politics:

> The Governor of the world places natural traits in the parts of the world by means of which they are made harmonious . . . like a single thing performing a single action for a single purpose. In the same manner, the governor of the nation must set down and prescribe voluntary traits and dispositions for the souls in the divisions of the nation and city that will bring them to that harmony . . . in such a way that . . . the nation and the nations become like a single thing performing a single action by which a single purpose is obtained. What corresponds to that becomes clear to anyone who contemplates the organs of the human body.[52]

In al-Fārābī's description, the individual providence effected by the first ruler should mirror God's general providence. Both tasks are compared to the body: Just as a human being's parts harmonize into a single organism, so does God harmonize the cosmos, and a first ruler harmonize the nation. I will have more to say about al-Fārābī's political *imitatio dei*, and how it compares to Maimonides' own, further on. For now, it is enough to note that while al-Fārābī's body-politic metaphor is Platonic, its practical upshot reflects the innovations of Islamic philosophy: a "common religion," one which "brings together [a people's] opinions, beliefs, and actions."[53]

Forging such a religion, and so removing the obstacles to popular happiness and divine rule, requires that a first ruler have two primary qualities. The first is "deliberative virtue" or "what the Ancients call 'prudence'": an ability to tailor philosophy's universal insights to the character, dispositions, lifeways, and experiences of a particular people.[54] Acquiring this faculty, al-Fārābī stresses, does not come through philosophical contemplation. It requires "experience arising from long involvement" in "single cities and nations."[55] To be a first ruler, in other words, a philosopher cannot just have theoretical insights. He has to spend time in the cave. Consequently, even holding philosophy constant, religion is going to look different based on its time, place, and context.[56] Yet

---

[52] *Religion*, 112.   [53] Plato, *Republic* (New York: Basic Books, 1991), 462d; *Religion*, 113.

[54] "There is a certain deliberative virtue that enables one to excel in the discovery of what is most useful for a virtuous end common to many nations, to a whole nation, or to a whole city, at a time when an event occurs that affects them in common. . . . This is the political deliberative virtue. . . . It is evident that the deliberative virtue with the highest authority can only be subordinated to the theoretical virtue; for it merely discerns the accidents of the intelligibles that, prior to having these accidents as their accompaniments, are acquired by the theoretical virtue" *Attainment of Happiness*, 64–67. See also *Religion*, 106–107.

[55] *Religion*, 107.

[56] *Political Regime*, 74–75. "The vulgar ought to comprehend merely the similitudes of [the ultimate principles], which should be established in their souls by persuasive arguments. One

such differences, for al-Fārābī, are consistent with universality. So long as a religion achieves social harmony toward the end of happiness, it is "virtuous," regardless of its particular laws, rituals, and practices.[57]

The first ruler's second virtue is excellence "in persuasion and in representing things through images" – that is, in "imagination."[58] Imagination is necessary because of the wide intellectual gap between philosophers and everyone else.[59] Consider the attainment of happiness. For a philosopher, gaining theoretical knowledge means developing his mind, via mastery of the sciences, to actualize his potential intellect, join the Active Intellect, and so receive emanation from the First Cause. For an ordinary person, however, such a framework is hopelessly abstract. He needs terms which personalize the deity and dramatize the experience. Thus instead of knowledge we have "revelation," coming from a state of spiritual elevation, via divine volition, to contact the "holy spirit," and so receive prophecy from God. Both descriptions, al-Fārābī argues, refer to one and the same experience. Yet from the first ruler's perspective, "the images and persuasive arguments are intended for others, whereas as far as he is concerned, these things are certain."[60] The philosopher, in other words, has demonstrative proofs for his ideas; others have "unexamined opinions": correct views about the conclusions of philosophy but without their underlying reasons.[61]

---

should draw a distinction between the similitudes that ought to be presented to every nation and not to another, to a particular city and not to another, or to a particular group among the citizens of a city and not to another. All these [persuasive arguments and similitudes] must be discerned by the deliberative virtue." *Attainment of Happiness*, 70. See also 63.

[57] *Religion*, 93–94.

[58] *Attainment of Happiness*, 77–78; *Political Regime*, 74. "Imagination," as understood by both al-Fārābī and Maimonides, refers to our ability to form images. It does not have the additional connotation of "free creativity" which we today, following the Romantics, often ascribe to it. *The Guide to the Perplexed*, trans. Lenn E. Goodman and Phillip Lieberman (Stanford: Stanford University Press, [1190] 2024), 161n447.

[59] *Philosophy of Aristotle*, 92–93; *Attainment of Happiness*, 70; *Political Regime*, 74.

[60] *Attainment of Happiness*, 79–80.

[61] *Attainment of Happiness*, 74–75; *Religion*, 97–98. "According to the ancients, religion is an imitation of philosophy. Both comprise the same subjects and both give an account of the ultimate end for the sake of which man is made – that is, supreme happiness – and the ultimate end of every one of the other beings. In everything of which philosophy gives an account based on intellectual perception or conception, religion gives an account based on imagination. In everything demonstrated by philosophy, religion employs persuasion." *Attainment of Happiness*, 77. See also 79–80. Al-Fārābī traces this idea – that theoretical knowledge can and should be translated into images for the benefit of the unlearned multitude – to Aristotle: "[Aristotle] gave an account of the art that enables man to project images of the things that became evident in the certain demonstrations in the theoretical arts, to imitate them by means of similitudes, and to project images of, and imitate, all the other particular things in which it is customary to employ images and imitation through speech. For image-making and imitation by means of similitudes is one way to instruct the multitude and the vulgar in a large number of difficult theoretical things so as to produce in their souls the impressions of these things by way of their similitudes." *Philosophy of Aristotle*, 92–93.

Did al-Fārābī truly seek to enlighten ordinary people and realize the rule of God? Or was his theocratic philosophy merely an elaborate ruse, a "rhetoric" of metaphysics to be deployed by a philosophical elite for securing obedience?[62] Strauss believed the latter. And in Strauss' view, this reading was shared by Maimonides and influenced him profoundly.[63] It is true that al-Fārābī was aware of an esoteric tradition of writing.[64] He did sometimes dissemble about what he actually believed.[65] Nonetheless, he appears earnest about his primary aims. Someone who fails to strive for happiness, for al-Fārābī, is not merely a misguided commoner; he has "sickness of soul" and should seek moral counsel.[66] The philosopher's theoretical knowledge takes priority; but he is also obligated to "facilitate instruction of the multitude."[67] And what the first ruler legislates is not merely his own arbitrary will. His intellect, perfectly realized through philosophy, is effectively indistinguishable from the Active Intellect. He is directly connected to what most people call God. The laws he makes are God's laws; his rule is God's rule.

Today we cannot but read al-Fārābī after Machiavelli, Dostoevsky, and Marx. Yet doing so may also tint our vision, turning what is undoubtedly a *paternalistic* project into an entirely *cynical* one. Indeed, Strauss, in his essay, seems to suggest that al-Fārābī was secretly channeling Nietzsche: "Al-Fārābī had rediscovered in the politics of Plato the golden mean equally removed from a naturalism which aims only at sanctioning the savage instincts of 'natural' man, the instincts of the master and the conqueror; and from a supernaturalism which tends to become the basis of slave morality."[68] Whatever al-Fārābī truly intended, I will argue in

---

[62] Joshua Parens, *Metaphysics as Rhetoric: Alfarabi's Summary of Plato's Laws* (Albany: SUNY Press, 1995).

[63] "To understand Maimonides, Farabi's view is much more important than Avicenna's. ... Maimonides expresses the opinion that prophecy is not a subject of speculative philosophy, but of practical or political philosophy." Strauss, "Remarks," 12–13.

[64] See Fraenkel, *Philosophical Religions*. To offer one example: "Although I have put these sciences and their well-guarded and sparely-revealed maxims in writing, I have nevertheless ordered them in such a manner that only those suited for them will get them, and I expressed them in an idiom only those adept in them will comprehend." *Religion*, 133. Moreover, as Jeffrey Macy has shown, al-Fārābī sometimes writes about the same subject in different ways, likely based on his intended or expected readership and its fidelity to traditional religious doctrine. For example, he does not consistently describe the first ruler as one who receives "revelation". See Macy, "A study in medieval Jewish and Arabic political philosophy: Maimonides' Shemonah Peraqim and al-Farabi's fusul al-madani (or fusul Muntaza'ah)," 38–46.

[65] See, for instance, al-Fārābī's invocation of the pseudo-*Theology of Aristotle* to defend the philosopher as a proponent of ex nihilo creation. "The Harmonization of the Two Opinions of the Two Sages: Plato the Divine and Aristotle," in *The Political Writings: "Selected Aphorisms" and Other Texts* (Ithaca: Cornell University Press, 2015), 155.

[66] *Political Regime*, 72.   [67] *Attainment of Happiness*, 74.

[68] "Remarks," 6. Strauss was self-described disciple of Nietzsche as a young adult. See for example Heinrich Meier, ed., *Gesammelte Schriften*, 3 Vols. (Stuttgart: J. B. Metzler, 1996–2001), 3: 648. Strauss' point in the passage quoted here seems to be that Nietzsche is right, but the philosopher

the rest of this study that Maimonides took his predecessor's theocratic project seriously. In al-Fārābī's thought, he saw both the desired end – the actualized rule of God – and the means of achieving it – the organization of society around the pursuit of happiness: theoretical knowledge for the philosophically adept, true beliefs for others. And as we have seen, the most important of these means, for al-Fārābī, is religion – or what he sometimes refers to, more simply, as "*law*."[69]

3 "Judgement Is God's": Law and Philosophy in Maimonides' *Commentary on the Mishnah*

Maimonides first hints at human beings' role in divine rule in a middle chapter of the introduction to his *Mishnah Commentary*.[70] He does not mention al-Fārābī by name in this work. But in a colophon at the *Commentary*'s conclusion, he notes that while composing it he had been actively studying philosophy and the sciences – a curriculum which would have surely included al-Fārābī. Maimonides' stated task in this section is to explain the Mishnah's structure: why certain tractates were placed where and what they are fundamentally about. Among the most well-known of these is *Pirkei Avot* [*Ethics of the Fathers*], an aphoristic text about ethical and pietistic virtues. One might expect to find *Avot* at the beginning or end of the Mishnah – as a framework for approaching the law or for making sense of its totality. Instead, it is located after tractates on civil law, the high court, and punishment. Why?

In answering, Maimonides draws a straight line between divine and human judgment:

> [*Avot* contains] a great ethical teaching for human beings: that they not say, "Why should we accept the judgment of person x or the ordinance of judge y?" In truth the matter is not like this, as judgment does not belong to judge y,

needs to make people believe that Nietzsche is not right. And this means creating a political order which prevents people from devouring one another, while simultaneously not imposing a "slave morality" which would make what Strauss calls a "truly critical philosophy" impossible.

[69] *Political Regime*, 70; *Religion*, 97.

[70] *Kitab al-Siraj [Book of the Lamp]*, begun when Maimonides was twenty-three and completed at thirty, was originally published in Arabic, but became popularly known by the title of its Hebrew translation, *Perush Ha-Mishna [Commentary on the Mishnah]*. For more on its translation history, see Hanoch Albeck, *Mavo La-Mishnah [Introduction to the Mishnah]* (Jerusalem: Bialik Institute, 1967). The Mishnah is the oldest layer of Judaism's oral law (in contrast to the written law of the Torah), transcribed in the centuries following the failed Second Revolt against Rome. It became the nucleus for the two Talmuds, texts developed in Babylonia (the "Talmud Bavli") and the land of Israel (the "Talmud Yerushalmi"), based on rabbinic hermeneutics, logic, and the incorporation of extra-Mishnaic texts, and assembled and redacted during roughly the sixth through ninth centuries CE. Moshe Halbertal notes that Maimonides' choice to treat the Mishnah as an independent object of study was highly unconventional, though that decision may be more explicable in light of his views of religious leadership, analyzed below. *Maimonides*, 92–94.

but rather to the Holy One, blessed be He, who commanded us about it, as it is stated (Deuteronomy 1:17), "for judgment is God's." Hence it is all one judgment, and they received it one man from another through the passing generations.[71]

Maimonides here is referring to *Avot*'s opening, which famously traces how the Torah, after being received by Moses at Mount Sinai, was transmitted to Joshua, the elders, the prophets, and each generation's leaders in a continuous chain. In a straightforward sense, then, the narrative is about the nature of the law: as revealed, and hence authoritative. This is how Maimonides reads it too. The text's first function, he writes, is "to inform that the consensus and the received tradition are true and correct."[72]

Yet in his gloss, Maimonides also quietly interpolates a more radical conclusion about judges themselves. When a judge adjudicates a point of Jewish law he is not merely doing his best to arrive at a correct ruling. In his capacity as judge, he is actually playing the part of God. His judgment *is* God's: "it is all one judgment." What we find here, therefore, is an echo of al-Fārābī's account of the dependence of divine rule on human rule. Just as a first ruler, for al-Fārābī, serves as a necessary agent of God's governance, so too, for Maimonides, does a judge. He is an instrument of divine will and wisdom.

Does Maimonides really mean that judges realize the rule of God? Here two objections might be raised. First, there is an important difference between the legal horizon faced by al-Fārābī's first ruler and any comparable figure in Maimonides' thought: the immutability of the law. For al-Fārābī, first rulers are made by philosophy, not chronology; while rare, they are not sui generis. And since the law expresses the first ruler's theoretical knowledge – shaped, via prudence, to the history and context of a given people – he, or a first ruler who follows him, can change it based on his judgment.[73] Maimonides, by contrast, repeatedly stresses both the Torah's permanence and Moses' incomparable status as legislator.[74] Second, one might suspect that Maimonides' words here

---

[71] Moses Maimonides, *Introduction to the Mishnah*, trans. Francis Nataf ([1168] 2017), 15:57–58. www.sefaria.org.

[72] *Introduction to the Mishnah*, 15:57.

[73] "Just as it is permissible for [a first ruler] to change a Law he legislated at one moment if he is of the opinion that it is more fitting to change it at another moment, so may the [first ruler] now present who succeeds the one who has passed away change what the one who has passed away has already legislated." *Political Regime*, 70.

[74] See for example *Guide*, 2:33–35, 2:39, 3:41; Moses Maimonides, "Introduction to Chelek," in *A Maimonides Reader*, ed. Isadore Twersky (New York: Behrman House, [1168] 1972); "Hilchot Melachim u-Milhamoteihem [Kings and Their Wars]," in *Mishneh Torah*, ed. Zvi. H. Preisler (Jerusalem: Ketuvim, [1180] 1993), 2:6; *Hilchot Teshuva [Repentance]*, 5:2, 9:2; "Hilchot Yesodei haTorah [Foundations of the Torah]," in *Mishneh Torah*, ed. by Zvi H. Preisler. (Jerusalem: Ketuvim, [1180] 1993), 1:10, 7:6, 8:1–3.

are meant metaphorically. By this view, he is doing something like what Carl Schmitt would later call 'political theology': drawing an analogy between judge and God in order to understand the former's role.[75] Schmitt thought the sovereign was *akin* to God, not an actual deity. Maimonides, accordingly, would be making a claim about the judge's authoritative position, not his ontological status.

Maimonides, I will now show, responds implicitly to both of these objections in his *Mishnah Commentary* introduction. To begin with, while the written law of the Torah is indeed fixed, the relative fluidity of the oral law permits moments of codification which, in practice, function as new foundings. The text of the law and its legal authority are retained. But changes can be effectively introduced in its interpretation and underlying rationale.[76] After concluding his catalogue of

---

[75] *Political Theology*, especially ch. 3.

[76] The fixity of the Torah text follows logically, for Maimonides, from its perfection (and the perfection of the lawgiver Moses). A perfect law could never be improved: "When a thing is perfect of its kind, anything else of the kind must be imperfect, going either too far or not far enough – just as any deviation from optimal balance of temper physiologically goes too far or not far enough. Our Torah is perfect in just this way, as its balance shows." *Guide*, 2:39. This argument is difficult to square, however, with Maimonides' view (which I discuss further on) that many of the Torah's laws were framed for their specific cultural and historical context. If that context changes, wouldn't those laws be rendered imperfect? Four additional reasons, never explicitly spelled-out by Maimonides, might be proposed for explaining the Torah's permanence. First, Maimonides is what we would today call a moral realist: He believes there are facts about God and facts about norms. Thus in so far as the Torah – or at least its theological and moral core – reflects facts of this kind, it cannot be changed. See for instance *Guide*, 1:2, 1:75, 3:15. Morality cannot be altered, even by God: "[God] and His throne [i.e. Justice] are inseparable." *Guide*, 1:9. See also 3:17. Still, one might respond that even for a moral realist, those laws whose moral implications are no longer relevant (e.g., mixing wool and linen) should be changeable. This suggests a second, more pragmatic reason: Those untutored in philosophy, and so unable to distinguish core moral truths from historically contingent practices, might come to believe that *all* of the Torah's claims are mutable, thereby undermining its authority. It thus becomes necessary to stress the permanence and perfection of the entire text. Maimonides in fact hints in this direction toward the end of the *Guide*: "Knowing that some rules of His law might need supplementation or suspension, as times, places, and circumstances change, God forbade adding or deleting any of them: *thou shalt not add to or diminish it* (Deuteronomy 13:1). For that would undermine the law and give color to the belief that it did not come from God. But God did allow the learned in every age – the High Court – to protect and preserve the Torah's precepts by introducing regulations to patch any gaps and to make such provisions permanent. . . . Regulated in this way, the Torah remains one and ever in effect, come what may." *Guide*, 3:41. See also Moses Maimonides, "Mitzvot Lo Ta'aseh [Negative Commandments]" in *Mishneh Torah*, ed. by Zvi H. Preisler. (Jerusalem: Ketuvim, [1180] 1993), §§366–70. Maimonides' concern here reflects a more general problem: When a law's authority is thought to be derived merely from reasons, as opposed to having a "higher," metaphysical, or sacred dimension, its authority evaporates if these reasons disappear – or if an individual decides that they don't apply to him. See my article "Democratic Solidarity in a Secular Age? Habermas and the 'Linguistification of the Sacred'," *The Journal of Politics* 81, no. 3 (2019). A third possible reason for the Torah's immutability directly parallels al-Fārābī: While al-Fārābī did allow for first rulers who succeeded the initial first ruler to change the law (see note 73), he did so with the caveat that if the initial first ruler approaches death and perceives no worthy successor, he may transcribe his legislation – seemingly oral, until this point – into a written form, at which point it replaces a human ruler's

the Mishnah's contents, Maimonides signals that Jewish history has seen three such founding moments, each associated with one of Israel's greatest figures:

> Rav Ashi secluded himself to compose the Talmud, and saw [fit] for himself to do for all the words of those that came after our Holy Rabbi [Judah the Prince] what our Holy Rabbi had done for the words of all that came after Moses.[77]

Moses established the written law; Judah the Prince compiled the oral law; and Rav Ashi composed the Babylonian Talmud.[78] One might think that the latter two cases were simply clarifications of what came earlier – that the law, once revealed, existed in its full form, and all that was needed was a reorganization. Yet when Maimonides had discussed the Mishnah's codification earlier in his introduction, he had noted a "secret" [sod] in the transmission of the oral law. "Explanations that were transmitted from the mouth of Moses have no disagreement about them in any way"; in all other cases, however, the law is a product of applying hermeneutic principles to the scriptural texts.[79] Only a fraction of the oral law, in other words, was given to Moses. The rest had to be created. Its present form is the result, in large part, of human reasoning.

On its own this might not seem especially remarkable; law, by its nature, must be interpreted. Yet since there are, in fact, very few oral laws which are untouched by disagreement, several important implications follow. First, the scope of the Sinai revelation narrows dramatically. What God gave Moses was limited: the written law, the oral law's general principles, and the means to

---

decrees as the basis for the city's governance: "When there does not happen to be a human being [worthy of replacing the initial first ruler], the Laws that the former [first ruler] prescribed or ordained are to be adopted, then written down and preserved, and the city is to be governed by means of them. So the ruler who governs the city by means of written Laws adopted from past leaders is the king of traditional law [*sunna*]." *Political Regime*, 70. Maimonides, who as I explore further on believed that the Torah was only written down in stages, hints at a similar view: "God . . . made it part of our nature that some of us are able to govern. Some, like a prophet or lawgiver, are inspired to rule. Others can implement or enforce what a prophet or lawgiver has laid down and instituted." *Guide*, 2:40. Finally, the Torah itself establishes its words as permanent, implying that even if its laws were malleable in philosophical principle, in practice their permanence is intrinsic to the text's authority: "It is a clear and manifest principle concerning the Torah that as a Law it is permanently established forever and evermore; and that it is not subject to mutability, nor to diminution, nor to amendment; for it is said: 'All this word which I command you, that shall ye observe to do; thou shalt not add thereto, nor diminish from it.'" *Hilchot Yesodei haTorah*, 9:1. See also Maimonides ' "Epistle to Yemen," in *Epistles of Maimonides*, ed. Abraham Halkin and David Hartman (Philadelphia: Jewish Publication Society, 1985).

[77] *Introduction to the Mishnah*, 16:6.

[78] It is still not known precisely when and by whom the Babylonian Talmud was finally redacted, but it was the work of many hands over several centuries. For an accessible introduction to and overview of rabbinic law, see Chaim N. Saiman, *Halakhah: The Rabbinic Idea of Law* (Princeton: Princeton University Press, 2018).

[79] *Introduction to the Mishnah*, 8:13.

extrapolate their details, along with a limited number of "laws of Moses from Sinai" which cannot be derived hermeneutically (like units of measure).[80] Second, the formation of Jewish law is now conceived as an essentially dynamic, creative, and agential process. As Maimonides remarks about the pre-Mishnaic period: "There was no time that there was not contemplation and innovation of the matters."[81] Or as he writes about the centuries before the Talmud's codification: "One generation after another did not cease from reflecting upon it, and investigating and explaining it."[82] Third, rational arguments, rather than claims to revelation, take center stage. The law unfolds through "research and reasoning"; decisions follow "the words of one thousand and one sages, not . . . the words of one thousand glorious prophets."[83] Fourth, laws can change, sometimes dramatically, between different codifications. Maimonides never states such a view explicitly. But he comes close in the *Guide* through his analysis of the *lex talionis*: "One who causes loss of a limb must lose the like member. . . . Don't worry that we [today, in rabbinic law,] assess damages here. My present aim is just to warrant the biblical laws, not our jurisprudence."[84]

These four implications point to a final and critical one: Moments of codification not only assemble and clarify the law but effectively *produce* it.[85] The Mishnah and Talmud both retain multiple legal views and reasonings. Yet by excluding certain opinions, and carefully curating others, the scope of juridical possibility is dramatically narrowed. The law is further specified. And in the process, jurisprudence is transformed and adapted for changed circumstances – something closely resembling what al-Fārābī called "prudence." Consider Maimonides' description in the *Mishneh Torah* of what motivated Judah the Prince's codification of the Mishnah: "Fresh calamities were continually

---

[80] *Introduction to the Mishnah*, 2:25, 8:23.   [81] *Introduction to the Mishnah*, 8:2.

[82] *Introduction to the Mishnah*, 16:5. In addition to changes introduced by changing the text's interpretation, Maimonides also observes the role of *takkanot* and *gezerot*, rabbinic decrees and safeguards which the High Court is authorized to legislate based on the authority granted to it by the Torah, but are not themselves stipulated by the Torah text. "Mitzvot Lo Ta'aseh," §369.

[83] *Introduction to the Mishnah*, 2:27, 7:47. As the Talmud itself puts it, "A Sage is even better than a prophet." Talmud Bavli, Tractate Bava Batra, 12a.

[84] *Guide*, 3:41. Maimonides offers a similar analysis regarding the command "let your camp by holy" (Deuteronomy 23:15). While rabbinic interpretation limits the scope of this law to the Temple precincts, Maimonides explains its rationale based on what he takes to be its original meaning: "So every soldier will see the camp as God's sanctuary, not like a gentile camp, devoted to sheer violence, rapine, pillage, and destruction. Our aim, rather, is to aid folk toward God's service and a better life. As I told you, I am warranting the commandments just as biblically stated." *Guide*, 3:41.

[85] Indeed Maimonides stresses that R. Ashi's purpose in redacting the Talmud was to establish (or reestablish) the law, to codify "the legal decision with one of the two disputants that disagreed about the words of the Mishnah." *Introduction to the Mishnah*, 16:10. For an extended discussion of this legal-historical process, see Moshe Halbertal, *People of the Book: Canon, Meaning, and Authority* (Cambridge, MA: Harvard University Press, 1997).

happening, the wicked Government was extending its domain and increasing in power, and Israelites were wandering and emigrating to distant countries. He therefore composed a work to serve as a handbook [lit. 'to be a hand for all']."[86] Yet the Mishnah was hardly just a handbook; it became, in effect, the law itself. The same is true with each subsequent codification: The new text, rather than the ebb and flow of oral argument, is transformed into the source of study and authority. The Sinai theophany becomes *one* founding moment – the most important, to be sure, in both philosophical principle and popular consciousness, but by no means the only one in the practical development of the law to Maimonides' day.[87]

Even with these remarkable powers, however, Judah the Prince and Rav Ashi are not yet first rulers in al-Fārābī's sense. They seem instead to embody what he called "jurists": unphilosophical successors to the first ruler who personify the religion's virtues, espouse its true beliefs, and faithfully apply the law.[88] Yet in continuing his *Mishnah Commentary* introduction, Maimonides suggests a deeper purpose for their projects, and with it, a deeper dimension to their nature. After offering three juridical reasons for Rav Ashi's composition of the Talmud – explaining disputes, rendering decisions, and justifying legal innovations – he turns to a fourth: including *derashot*, parables. These stories, Maimonides is quick to clarify, are not merely homilies. "When one observes these narratives with intellectual observation, [matters] of the true good – about which there is nothing higher – are understood from them. And from them are

---

[86] *Hakdama [Introduction]*, 15.

[87] Indeed Maimonides likely saw himself as effecting just such a founding with his *Mishneh Torah*, redirecting the focus of study from the Mishnah and Talmud to his own legal code. See Halbertal, *Maimonides*, ch. 4. Maimonides implicitly compares himself to Judah the Prince in the *Guide*, invoking the same modified passage from Psalms that his predecessor did in justifying the transcription of the Oral Law: "*The time has come to act for the Lord* (Psalms 119:126, quoted at B. Berachot 63a)." *Guide*, Advice about this Work. Parallel to Maimonides, al-Fārābī had argued in *Religion* that subsequent first rulers may find the need to change the law not because of an error made by the initial first ruler, but because of changing historical conditions, a reflection of the first ruler's virtue of "prudence." Were the initial first ruler still governing, al-Fārābī suggests, he too would have made such changes: "[The initial first ruler] made a determination according to what was best for his time and this [later] one makes a determination according to what is best subsequent to the time of the first, this being the kind of thing the [initial first ruler] would alter also, were he to observe it." *Religion*, 99.

[88] *Religion*, 99–101. See also al-Fārābī's description of a "ruler of the tradition," in contrast to a first ruler: "[Political science explains] that virtuous rulership is of two types: a first rulership and a rulership dependent on it. First rulership is the one that establishes the virtuous ways of life and dispositions in the city or nation without their having existed among the people before that, and it converts them from the ignorant ways of life to the virtuous ways of life. The person undertaking this rulership is the first ruler. The rulership dependent on the first is the one that follows in the steps of the first rulership with regard to its actions. The one who undertakes this rulership is called ruler of the tradition and king of the tradition. His rulership is based on an existing tradition." *Religion*, 104.

revealed theological matters and true things … that the philosophers attained over the generations."[89] Foremost among these matters: The "*Ma'aseh Bereshit*" and the "*Ma'aseh Merkavah*" – what he will later identify, in the *Guide*, with physics and metaphysics.[90] Here the echoes of al-Fārābī begin to grow louder. The sages, Maimonides seems to imply, were not merely jurists. They were philosophers.

4 "The Holy One Has in His World Only the Four Cubits of the Law": Knowledge, Providence, and Human Agency

Rav Ashi's inclusion of *derashot* becomes a springboard for Maimonides to launch a lengthy digression on the centrality of philosophy for religious leadership. Israel's sages, he argues, devoted every effort to pursuing theoretical knowledge – what al-Fārābī called "happiness." And like al-Fārābī's first rulers, they used their imaginations: They embedded philosophical insights into parables, hinting at truths without prompting the masses, "according to the shortcomings of their natures," to recoil from philosophy's rigors.[91] The greatest of Israel's sages were thus masters of both law and philosophy – instruments of God's governance.

Maimonides prefaces his discussion by citing a well-known saying from the Talmud, Tractate Berachot: "The Holy One, blessed be He, only has in His world the four cubits of the law (*halacha*) alone."[92] Standardly interpreted, this aphorism stresses the centrality of Torah study: God cannot be apprehended like the world's other phenomena, so if you want to know Him, study His law. For Maimonides, however, such a reading cannot be correct. It implies that in the pre-Sinaitic age "there was no share to the Holy One," that "the law alone [is] the appropriate focus and the other wisdoms and traits are thrown behind His back."[93] And the truth is just the opposite. The Sages, Maimonides insists, actually saw other disciplines merely as steps "through which to get to theology."[94] The latter was their chief occupation, something to "pore over" night and day, the "end of wisdom."[95] It is only because such "wisdom has disappeared" from Israel that philosophy's true import, and central place in Torah, is no longer recognized.[96] The passage from Berachot must therefore be

---

[89] *Introduction to the Mishnah*, 16:14.
[90] *Introduction to the Mishnah*, 16:17; *Guide*, 1: Introduction.
[91] *Introduction to the Mishnah*, 16:16.
[92] *Introduction to the Mishnah*, 16:41. See Talmud Bavli, Tractate Berachot, 8a.
[93] *Introduction to the Mishnah*, 16:41.   [94] *Introduction to the Mishnah*, 16:34.
[95] *Introduction to the Mishnah*, 16:40.
[96] *Introduction to the Mishnah*, 16:37. Maimonides reiterates this point in the *Guide* in describing the conditions of exile: "Bred up in superstition, we found philosophy foreign to our Torah." *Guide*, 2:11. See also 1:71.

read another way: "But if you investigate this matter intellectually, you will see in it a wonderful thing from the wisdoms. . . . And I will elucidate them for you in order that it be an example for the rest of what comes to your hand. And hence, place your heart to it as is fit."[97]

Maimonides' words, still oblique, become intelligible as he unfolds his analysis in the next chapter. His discussion centers around teleology and "the ancients," a likely reference to Aristotle.[98] These philosophers, he writes, saw man's ultimate end as the comprehension of "intellectual secrets" – a movement from the potential to actual intellect.[99] And "the most honored of the ideas," he continues, is "the unity of the Holy One . . . knowledge of Divinity."[100] Yet contemplation is not man's only *telos*. The "purpose of the world," Maimonides writes, is a man who is not only "wise" but "good."[101] He then explains his meaning:

> When it becomes clear to a man that he is from the type of men that are of mind and deed – I mean to say with mind, to depict with his intellect the truth of things according to what they are, and to grasp all that is possible for a man to grasp; and the deed is the *tikkun* and *yoshar* of the natural things . . . and so, the man that accords with this is the purpose and the aspiration. And this thing is not known only from the prophets, but the sages of the transitory nations . . . they too already knew that a man is not complete unless he encompasses mind and deed.[102]

Tikkun is a form of the verb *le-taken*, which literally means "repair," "correct," or "set right." But readers familiar with Maimonides' later writings will recall another place where he invokes the term: the *Mishneh Torah*'s "Laws of Kings and their Wars." *Le-taken ha-'olam* is the activity by which Israel's kings establish public order and justice.[103] It is also the activity which identifies the true messiah – a man who brings the whole world to know and serve God: "He arranges the whole world [*le-taken et ha-'olam kulo*] to serve God as one."[104] *Yoshar*, from the root for "straightness," connotes integrity, honesty, and equity. And Maimonides, notably, uses the word only one other time in his *Mishnah Commentary* introduction: to describe the ideal judge, whose rulings should be "acts of *yoshar*."[105]

Maimonides thus brings us full circle. "The four cubits of the law" are not means by which we know God. They are means for turning us – or more

---

[97] *Introduction to the Mishnah*, 16:42.   [98] *Introduction to the Mishnah*, 17:1.
[99] *Introduction to the Mishnah*, 17:19.   [100] *Introduction to the Mishnah*, 17:21.
[101] *Introduction to the Mishnah*, 17:24.   [102] *Introduction to the Mishnah*, 17:25.
[103] *Hilchot Melachim*, 3:10.   [104] *Hilchot Melachim*, 11:7.
[105] *Introduction to the Mishnah*, 15:70. The connection Maimonides makes here between wisdom and action, and his allusion to Aristotle, echoes al-Fārābī's "harmonization" of Plato and Aristotle. *Harmonization*, 129–30. See also *Philosophy of Plato*, 60.

precisely, those human beings who acquire knowledge of the deity through physics, metaphysics, and theology – into *agents* of God. Just as in al-Fārābī (a "sage of the transitory nations") true philosophy manifests in action: the "kingly craft" of religion, and especially, religious law. In Maimonides' earlier metaphor, "heart" – what we would call "mind" – will extend one's "hand" – a metaphor for "deed." It will lead to *tikkun* and *yoshar*, actions which bring order and harmony to the world. When fully developed, therefore, human judgment for Maimonides is not only akin to God's judgment; it *is* His judgment. God rules the world through virtuous laws made, interpreted, and applied by exceptionally wise human beings – those who have achieved a measure of providence.

Indeed Maimonides, fittingly, concludes his discussion by returning to Rav Ashi. After noting that he has "digressed from the matter we were involved in," Maimonides explains that it was nonetheless valuable to "edify the faith and stimulate the pursuit of wisdom."[106] And then he describes Rav Ashi's completion of the Talmud: "The greatness of his composition and its powerful utility were testimony that the spirit of the Holy God was in him."[107] Rav Ashi, we are meant to infer, was not only a jurist but a true philosopher. While he did not change the law, he did refound the nation. He was a first ruler for Israel.

In his *Mishnah Commentary*, Maimonides does not give us a complete picture of how theoretical knowledge produces this kind of providential agency. A discussion of such theological details, he writes, would be "very lengthy."[108] We, however, can fill them in from later texts, and especially from the *Guide*.[109] Through emanation, God exercises His direct providence over the intellects and spheres and His general providence over nature.[110] But "in His *world*," the

---

[106] *Introduction to the Mishnah*, 17:49.   [107] *Introduction to the Mishnah*, 17:50.

[108] *Introduction to the Mishnah*, 17:21.

[109] Maimonides, as copies of his writings from the Cairo Geniza have shown, was continually revising his work and refining his thought. See Halbertal, *Maimonides*, 92–94. There are differences between his views in the *Mishnah Commentary* and *Guide*, as for example whether the world and its contents should be understood as having been created for the sake of human beings. *Introduction to the Mishnah*, 17:32–47; *Guide*, 3:13. Even so, the two texts are substantially consistent in philosophical approach.

[110] Referring to God's governance of the spheres specifically, Maimonides reads emanationist ideas into biblical verses, while stressing God's ultimate volition against Neoplatonic assertions of divine necessity: "We read of God *riding the heavens to your aid* (Deuteronomy 33.26) – controlling them. Similarly, *who rides the `aravot* (Psalms 68:5), ruling the `aravot, i.e., the topmost sphere. . . . The rider spurs his beast and guides it as he likes, as an instrument of his will. But he does not depend on it and is not in direct contact with it but separate. Just so, God moves the highest sphere, by whose motion all within is moved, yet He is apart from it, not a force within it. . . . Reflect on this, and you'll see how [the Sages] explain God makes the sphere His instrument in governing the world." *Guide*, 1:70. He likewise describes the function of the heavenly bodies in the language of emanation and rule a few chapters later: "All the Philosophers agree that governance of the world here below is effected by powers emanating

achievement of individual providence is up to us. It depends on the extent to which we develop our rational faculties, attain the Active Intellect, and so receive the stream of divine emanation:

> Providence, in my belief, depends on reason, and reason is its measure. For it flows from a Mind of consummate perfection. Anyone touched by that flow so as to attain reason is, to that extent, reached by providence.[111]

As in al-Fārābī, emanation thus plays a key role in Maimonides' understanding of both knowledge and providence. By emanating the forms, God creates and continually sustains the world. And when we use our reason to form true ideas or concepts about the world – when our subjective apprehension rises to the level of truth and objectivity – we apprehend nature, in effect, just as God does.[112] We call this "revelation"[113]

The existence and extent of our providential agency, in turn, depends on the quality of our knowledge, something Maimonides stresses in a well-known discussion in the *Guide* of free will. In a chapter about which he tells us to give

---

from the sphere. ... The Torah, too, says so explicitly ... *to rule by day and by night, and divide* ... (Genesis 1:18). Rule here is delegated authority; it's not just about light and darkness." *Guide*, 2:5. Maimonides also explains emanation in more general terms: "The action of bodies on one another through their forms must be in predisposing matter for the impact of the non-physical causes that are the forms. The work of the Active Intellect is manifest in the world, in everything new that does not arise from mere mingling of bodies. And since this cause is non-physical, we know of necessity that it does not act by contact or at a distance, since it is not a body. So its action is called the flow of emanation, likening it to a spring ever flowing from all sides, drawn from no one quarter but spreading everywhere, ever gushing forth to all things in all direction, near and far. Just so is this Mind untouched by any force from anywhere or at any distance, but its effects reach all it touches, from no one quarter, at no specific remove and no specific time. Its action is constant, so long as anything is fit to receive its constant influence, the so-called flow of emanation. Likewise the creator. Since it is demonstrated that He is not a body and established that the universe is His work, and He its active Cause, as I've explained and shall explain further, the world is said to emanate from Him, and all that arises in it is said to spring from Him. And in the same way, He is said to shed His wisdom on the Prophets. What all this means is that these are the acts of an incorporeal being. This is what is called emanation." *Guide*, 2:12. See also *Introduction to Chelek*.

[111] *Guide*, 3:17. As Maimonides put it elsewhere in the same chapter, "Divine providence, as I see it, comes only by emanation. The only species touched by this intellectual outflow and so given reason and made aware of all that a mind can reveal is the one attended by providence." Earlier in the text he had connected emanation even more directly to human governance: "Nature is such, you should realize, that the divine emanation reaching us enables us to think, and some to think better than others. For it may flow more fully to one person than to another. To one it may suffice for his enlightenment alone. Or, like anything else, it might spill over beyond what that one person's perfection requires and foster that of others. Some grow enlightened enough to govern others; some, just enough to be governed." Maimonides then suggests that we can distinguish between different notable classes in society – "scholars," "prophets," and "statesmen" – based the quantity and direction of the emanative flow they receive. *Guide*, 2:37. See also 3:18, where Maimonides describes how individual providence varies with a person's "share in divine reason's emanation."

[112] *Guide*, 2:4.   [113] *Guide*, 1:46.

"special attention, beyond any other," Maimonides explains that while many causes are "ascribed scripturally to God," in truth the deity delegates causation to both supernal and human forces: the intellects ("angels") for nature, and free will for human beings. God, Maimonides writes, "imposed that choice on this rational animal."[114] Readers who were influenced by Strauss, including translator Shlomo Pines, saw this phrase as Maimonides' covert rejection of free will – a hint that even our apparently free choices can be traced, causally, back to God. Accordingly, he renders the relevant words as "necessitated this particular free choice."[115] As Lenn Goodman demonstrates, however, this misconstrues the Arabic. Maimonides here follows Aristotle's distinction between two forms of agential actions: those that are "voluntary" by virtue of stemming from our will (a capacity we share with animals), and those that are genuinely free because they reflect rational choice.[116] Thus what God "necessitated" was not *what* we decided. It was *that we need to decide freely*. Far from denying free will, Maimonides actually insists that human beings cannot but choose freely, with the quality of our choices depending on the caliber of our reason.[117] Reason, as we have seen, is itself of divine provenance via emanation.[118] And so individual providence, reflected in our free choices, differs based on the extent of one's rational development: "It varies with our perfection as human beings."[119]

---

[114] *Guide*, 2:48.

[115] Moses Maimonides, *The Guide of the Perplexed, Volume 2*, trans. Shlomo Pines (Chicago: The University of Chicago Press, [1190] 1974), 2:48.

[116] *Guide*, 2:48, n. 424.

[117] Maimonides insists that human beings almost always cause their own misfortunes, inflicting them either on others or themselves. *Guide*, 3:12. They are likewise responsible for their own redemption, as he stresses in his introduction to *Pirkei Avot*: "The remedy for this disease [i.e. sin] is in our hands, for, as our misdeeds were the results of our own free will, we have, likewise, the power to repent of our evil deeds." *Introduction to Pirkei Avot [Ethics of the Fathers]*, trans. Joseph I. Gorfinkle ([1168] 1966), 8:7. www.sefaria.org. See also his well-known phrasing from his tractate on "Repentance [*Hilchot Teshuva*]" in the *Mishneh Torah*: "Every human being may become righteous like Moses, our teacher, or wicked, like Jeroboam. . . . There is no one that coerces him or decrees what he is to do, or draws him to either of the two ways; but every person turns to the way he desires, spontaneously and of his own volition." *Hilchot Teshuva*, 5:2. In the *Guide*, these ideas underly his reading of the account of Adam and Eve's eating from the Tree of Knowledge. Contrary to popular misconceptions, Maimonides argues, human beings had moral freedom *prior* to being tested by the serpent. Moreover, they had access to correct ideas of good and evil via their divinely given rational faculties: "Reason, shed by God on man by way of emanation, is indeed our highest attainment. But this Adam had before he disobeyed. That is why he was said to be in God's *image* and *likeness* ([Genesis] 1:26) – and why he could be addressed and given duties, as it says, *the Lord God commanded* . . . (2:16). Beasts receive precepts, nor does anyone who lacks reason." *Guide*, 1:2. It makes no sense for a just God to give a command to one who cannot follow it. Prelapsarian human beings must have had both access to knowledge of good and evil and the ability to act on it.

[118] *Guide*, 3:17.   [119] *Guide*, 3:18.

Just as for al-Fārābī, therefore, for Maimonides divine rule depends on human knowledge. The deity governs both heaven and earth. But he governs the latter in "another way": through us. Just as God delegates cosmic governance to the spheres, he delegates self-governance to us via our free will. The greater our knowledge of God, the more providence we have.[120] The more providence we have, the more our actions can be said to reflect God's wisdom. And insofar as our actions reflect God's wisdom, God can be said to rule. Maimonides alludes to this idea later in his *Mishnah Commentary*, in his essay on *Avot* itself ("Eight Chapters"). A man's goal, he writes, should be to "subordinate all the faculties of his soul to reason"; he should "keep his mind's eye fixed constantly upon one goal, namely, the attainment of the knowledge of God."[121] Yet such knowledge is not idle. For Maimonides, quoting *Avot*, it manifests in action: "Let all your deeds be for the sake of heaven."[122] Commonly interpreted, this aphorism is about piety and intention: A person should strive to do the right thing for the right reasons. But we are now positioned to read it differently. For when our actions are the result of true knowledge, Maimonides has shown us, they are not ours alone. They are "for the sake of heaven" – contributions to a theocratic project. They amount, in effect, to the governance of God.

5 "God Governs This World by Way of Angels": Moses in the *Guide to the Perplexed*

The bond Maimonides forges between philosophy, action, and divine rule has implications well beyond his *Mishnah Commentary*. Foremost among them are his views on leadership. This is especially true in the *Guide*, where, as a number of scholars have observed, Maimonides depicts Moses in a form closely resembling al-Fārābī's first ruler and Plato's philosopher king.[123] For Strauss, Maimonides' Moses is a "philosopher and statesman . . . and at the same time a diviner and magician."[124] His mode is "Platonic politics": the imposition of a law to achieve obedience for the many and free inquiry for the few.[125]

---

[120] Elsewhere in his *Mishnah Commentary*, Maimonides affirms that true belief is sufficient for one's intellect to achieve a measure of immortality. He can thereby reconcile his own intellectualist understanding of life after death with the Talmud's statement, "All Israel have a portion in the world to come." Talmud Bavli, Tractate Sanhedrin, 90a. See *Introduction to Chelek*. But as he indicates in the *Guide*, attaining individual providence has a higher bar, requiring theoretical knowledge grounded in reasons. *Guide*, 3:17.

[121] *Introduction to Pirkei Avot [Ethics of the Fathers]*, 5:1.

[122] *Introduction to Pirkei Avot [Ethics of the Fathers]*, 5:8; Mishnah, Tractate Pirkei Avot: 2:12.

[123] See for example Melamed, *Philosopher-King*; Aviezer Ravitzky, "Philosophy and Leadership in Maimonides," in *Maimonides after 800 Years: Essays on Maimonides and His Influence*, ed. Jay M. Harris (Cambridge, MA: Harvard University Press, 2007).

[124] "Remarks," 13.   [125] "Remarks," 5–6.

Non-Straussian readings, by contrast, tend to stress his pedagogical role. Maimonides' Moses becomes a kind of mirror for Maimonides himself, a figure who, by virtue of his unparalleled cognitive attainments, is uniquely positioned to lead his people to greater knowledge of God.[126] What have been passed over between these two appraisals, and what I will seek to bring out here, are his specifically theocratic dimensions. For Maimonides, Moses not only sought to bring Israel to true beliefs about God. He aimed to transform it, as a nation, into an instrument for divine rule.

Maimonides signals Moses' singular role by reimagining him as an "angel." "Angels" may be foreign to today's political thought but they are a central to Maimonides' scheme for delegating divine governance. The Muslim dialectical theologians (*mutakallimūn*) fervently shielded the deity's omnipotence by asserting His miraculous volition over all of reality. They eliminated the natural order.[127] Maimonides, by contrast, argues that God governs the world through the forces of nature. In philosophy, these forces are the Neoplatonic intellects: incorporeal agents which rotate the sphere, regulate the seasons, and function as what we might call natural laws. In the Bible, they are angels.[128] Maimonides notes, however, that angels can also be people: "You can see how an angel might be a human messenger. . . . And the word is applied to prophets. . . . *He sent His*

---

[126] Hermann Cohen, *Ethics of Maimonides*, trans. Almut Sh. Bruckstein (Madison: University of Wisconsin Press, [1908] 2004); J. J. Guttmann, *Dat u-madda [Science and religion]* (Jerusalem: Magnes Press, 1955); Menachem Kellner, *Maimonides on Human Perfection* (Atlanta: Scholars Press, 1990); Joseph B. Soloveitchik, *Maimonides: Between Philosophy and Halakhah*, ed. Lawrence J. Kaplan (New York: KTAV, [1950–51] 2016).

[127] The *mutakallimūn* occasionalists fail to distinguish between natural and logical possibility, giving God the ability to overturn not only natural laws but logical and moral truths. The philosophers take the opposite stance, arguing that the world could not have been other than it is. Maimonides' adopts a position between them: He affirms God's voluntaristic control over nature – contending, for instance, that the stars could have been placed differently, and affirming the possibility of ex nihilo creation; but he rejects God's power over logic or morality. *Guide*, 1:71, 1:73, 2:17, 2:19. Maimonides also criticizes the *mutakallimūn* more generally for their stance toward reason and tradition. True philosophers follow "wherever the argument, like the wind, tends." Plato, *Republic*, 394d. The *mutakallimūn* apologists, by contrast, begin with uncontestable claims based on revelation or traditional authority (such as ex nihilo creation) and then marshal arguments to achieve their desiderata, "pretend[ing] that reason alone had brought them to these conclusions." Maimonides completely rejects this knowledge orientation: "When I reflected on this approach, my soul recoiled violently, and rightly so." And he makes plain where he stands: "In a word, I say, as Themistius did, that reality does not conform to our ideas; true ideas must conform to reality." *Guide*, 1:71. See also 2:47. As he puts it in his *Mishnah Commentary*, those who accept the primacy of reason "are convinced of the impossibility of the impossible and the necessary existence of what must exist." *Introduction to Chelek*. See also his dismissal of astrology in his *Letter to Yemen*, on the grounds that "its postulates can be refuted by real proofs on rational grounds."

[128] At the same time, Maimonides – against a number of pre-Islamic Neoplatonists – argues that the angels/intellects are not themselves gods, but creations of God: "[Angels] are incorporeal minds, but only creatures, made by God." *Guide*, 1:49.

angel and brought us out of Egypt (Numbers 20:16)."[129] In its original context, these words are conveyed by Moses to the people of Edom as part of a plea to transit their territory. A plain reading of the passage thus suggests that the "angel" is one of the supernal beings who helped redeem Israel – the "angel of death" or the "pillar of fire." Yet Maimonides subtly, but unmistakably, wants us to identify him as a prophet: *Moses himself.* What are the stakes here?

At issue is nothing less than the crux of theocracy itself: whether any human government can truly serve as an extension of God's rule. The question hinges on the relationship we have seen between free will, reason, and providence. Not only human beings but also the intellects, Maimonides argues, are conscious agents. They "know what they do and use will and choice in exercising the powers of governance God gives them by emanation, just as we can voluntarily in what emanation empowers us to do." Even so, their choices are "not like ours." Whereas human beings frequently err, angels, in the fullness of their reason, always decide correctly. Whereas human choices concern "transient events," angelic ones regard permanent things, like the motions of the cosmos.[130] Yet this contrast raises a serious problem: How can a revealed law reflect God's infinite wisdom rather than one person's partial wisdom? By what means can it realize God's just rule rather one person's arbitrary rule? Maimonides' answer is to again turn Moses into an angel. Ostensibly referring to the intellects, he quotes from Exodus: "*Heed him, harken to his voice. Do not defy him. He will brook no trespass from you. For My name is in him* (Exodus 23:20–21)."[131] The verse right before the quoted passage clarifies that the "him" is an "angel" (*malach*). It also strongly implies that this angel is Moses. Moses, we thus learn, did not have free will in the way that others do. Like the intellects, it was also involved in 'exercising the powers of governance' given to him by God.

The theocratic implications of Maimonides' comparison emerge even more strongly in light of his theory of prophecy. A prophet disseminates philosophical truths: He translates the emanative flow of ideas he receives from the Active Intellect into accessible words, symbols, and exhortations.[132] Yet Moses' prophecy, Maimonides repeatedly stresses, was different. He grasped God's purpose "unmediated by the imagination."[133] He "attained to the angelic rank

---

[129] *Guide*, 2:6.   [130] *Guide*, 2:7.   [131] *Guide*, 2:7.

[132] *Guide*, 2:32–38, 2:47. Maimonides describes "ordinary" (non-Mosaic) prophecy in this way: "Prophecy, you see, in essence, is really an emanation flowing from God by way of the Active Intellect, first to the faculty of reason and on to that of imagination." The content of non-Mosaic prophecy, he emphasizes, is thus poetic and eidetic: "God tells us here what prophecy really is in essence: an attainment reached through a dream or vision. The word 'vision' (*mar'ah*) derives from *ra'ah*, to see. Imagination works so well that it pictures things as though they were before us, the image it presents seeming to come from the senses." *Guide*, 2:36. See also *Introduction to Chelek.*

[133] *Guide*, 2:45.

and became included in the order of the angels ... he remained a pure intellect only."[134] And this suggests a startling conclusion. In *Religion*, al-Fārābī had compared the first ruler's task in harmonizing his people with God's in harmonizing the world. "What corresponds to that," he wrote, "becomes clear to anyone who contemplates the organs of the human body."[135] In the middle of his discussion of angels, Maimonides uses the same example of bodily organs.[136] And he highlights the role of one angel in particular: the "Active Intellect ... the angel, 'vice-regent of the world' constantly cited by the Sages" and from whom "all forms stem."[137] The implication is plain: Moses was no ordinary angel. Elevated to the "rank" of the intellects, he too was a "vice-regent" of God. He was positioned to govern the human world in the same way that the Active Intellect governs the natural world. Likewise, consider how Maimonides, after another oblique scriptural reference to Moses, describes the angels ascending and descending Jacob's ladder in the mold of Plato's philosopher kings: "After rising to a certain rung comes descent with what was gained, to govern and teach those on earth."[138] Moses was not only *connected* to the Active Intellect; he was *fused* with it. Everything he thought and did – the whole content of the Torah – directly channeled divine wisdom. Moses wrote the law; God dictated. Moses legislated; God governed.[139]

6 "This Law Is Divine": The Torah as "Kingly Craft"

By placing Moses on par with the incorporeal intellects, Maimonides can ascribe angelic qualities to the Mosaic legislation: Just as angels' acts are "ever good," so are the Torah's laws; just as angels deal in permanent things, so will the Torah never be replaced. In this way, he can intimate how Moses' "kingly craft" – the Torah itself – surmounts each of the obstacles to realizing theocracy outlined by al-Fārābī: harmonizing society, rendering philosophy's insights accessible, and adapting universal ideas for particular contexts. Put another way, in the *Guide* Maimonides applies the same Farabian template to the Bible that he had to rabbinic texts in the *Mishnah Commentary*. He shows how it harbors both philosophical truths and practical means for realizing divine rule.

---

[134] *Introduction to Chelek.*   [135] *Religion*, 112.
[136] Maimonides had earlier expounded on the organ analogy in terms very closely matching al-Fārābī's: "Just as the human body has organs that rule and others that are ruled, dependent for their survival on the governing organ, the world as a whole has ruling parts." *Guide*, 1:72.
[137] *Guide*, 2:6.   [138] *Guide*, 1:15; Plato, *Republic*, 519c–20c.
[139] Compare al-Fārābī: "When the human intellect achieves its ultimate perfection, its substance comes close to being the substance of this intellect. ... [The Active Intellect] is intellected by man only when he is not separated from it by an intermediary. In this way, the soul of man itself becomes this Intellect." *Philosophy of Aristotle*, 127.

The initial obstacle a first ruler must overcome is forging a social unity directed at "happiness" – that is, knowledge of God. Most human governments, Maimonides argues, only strive to create order. They care "not a whit if people's views are sick or sound," but are "concerned only to manage relations in whatever way the ruler thinks promotes happiness as he sees."[140] A government based on revealed law, by contrast, is also directed toward higher things. Its norms not only secure "bodily welfare" but impart "wholesome beliefs" and "sound views, first about God and then about the angels." The law's vital aim, in other words, is to cultivate true beliefs, or ideally theoretical knowledge: People should hold accurate ideas about the divine realm; if they are able, they can then seek out the rational foundations for these ideas. When legislation is so oriented, one can be assured "this law is divine."[141]

Governance thus occupies an invaluable place in Maimonides' broader teleological understanding of human activities. Unlike Aristotle, who describes the *polis* as part of nature, Maimonides emphasizes that "law is not natural." It responds to a paradox: On the one hand, we cannot subsist on our own; on the other, our natural differences generate antagonism.[142] The law's most essential function, therefore, is to create a homogenized layer of shared norms and conventions to smooth our unsociability into "well-ordered community."[143] Inhabitants of law-governed societies can begin the next stage of human development: cultivating moral virtue. Maimonides details these virtues in a number of places, including most famously in the *Mishneh Torah*'s tractate on "Human Dispositions" [*Hilchhot De'ot*]. In the *Guide*, he divides them into three categories: quelling the appetites and passions; cultivating gentleness and amiability; and achieving purity, sanctity, and holiness.[144] Yet like social order, moral growth of this kind is only instrumentally valuable. Humanity's highest rung, "our true end as human beings," is philosophy: the "contemplation of ideas, the highest and most lasting being of God and the angels."[145]

---

[140] Very similar in description is al-Fārābī's "necessary city," which sets as its end human material needs but has no concern for cultivating the soul. *Political Regime*, 77.

[141] *Guide*, 2:40.

[142] al-Fārābī likewise argues that human beings need one another in order to "complete their necessary affairs" and "gain their most excellent state." *Political Regime*, 60. For an analysis of other potential causes of social dissolution, see my article "What Undermines Solidarity? Four Approaches and their Implications for Contemporary Political Theory," *Critical Review of International Social and Political Philosophy* 21, no. 5 (2018).

[143] *Guide*, 2:40.

[144] *Guide*, 3:33. Maimonides frequently stresses that the point of a Torah command is not simply to do the command, but to acquire its corresponding virtue or virtues. Consider how he describes the rationale behind the law to return lost property: "It fosters virtue, improves relations, and promotes reciprocity. If you don't return what someone lost, you won't get back what you lost – just as, if you fail to honor your father, your son won't honor you." *Guide*, 3:40. See also 3:52.

[145] *Guide*, 3:8. Maimonides here closely tracks al-Fārābī's definition of political science: "Knowing the things by which the citizens of cities attain happiness through political

Accomplishing this end poses a problem, however: Most people are not capable of philosophy.[146] Like al-Fārābī, Maimonides separates the intellectually adept from the unlearned masses. And while the fixity of this division is a matter of interpretive debate, the stakes, as we have seen, are not merely personal – whether this or that individual will develop fully – but collective and political, a point he hints at in citing al-Fārābī's lost commentary on Aristotle's *Nicomachean Ethics*: "It is those able to advance morally that Plato said enjoy more of God's providence."[147] The path leading from political order to moral virtue to divine knowledge, in other words, is about more than just wisdom. It is about achieving individual "providence" – "God's governance by another way." Disseminating philosophy, at a national scale, serves the ends of theocracy. Means must therefore be found to make theoretical ideas accessible to the masses.

Maimonides finds these means in the Torah itself. He sees the Torah's language as reflecting, in effect, the end product of a Farabian first ruler's imaginative faculty. It codes philosophical knowledge in religious forms like words, symbols, and images:

> The Torah "speaks in human language" . . . because it's meant to be accessible and studied by young people, women, and ordinary folk, without the capacity to understand things as they really are. Of them no more is asked than faith in whatever sound beliefs are best for them to hold. . . . As one matures and "the Torah's mysteries are opened up to him" (B. Hagigah 13a), by another or by his own efforts . . . one will be able to affirm these truths more properly, proving what can be proved, or using the best arguments possible. At that point one conceives and grasps as realities what were once just images and poetry for him.[148]

Maimonides never credits such images to Moses; he always attributes them to the Torah itself, or to God. Yet those familiar with philosophy – as Maimonides

---

association in the measure that innate disposition equips each of them for it." *Attainment of Happiness*, 61.

[146] *Guide*, 1: Introduction, 1:17, 1:33–34, 3:27–28.   [147] *Guide*, 3:18.

[148] *Guide*, 1:33. While here Maimonides seems to suggest that any human being, in principle, could acquire genuine knowledge, elsewhere he indicates his belief in an innate – and largely immutable – intellectual hierarchy: "Intellectual acuity, too, varies greatly from one person to the next. This too is clear and evident to scholars. One person might independently discover an idea that someone else would never understand, no matter how it was explained to him. Even if spelled out at length with all sorts of paraphrases and examples, his mind would not penetrate it but just glance off." Maimonides notes that such "deficits of human understanding" were also "familiar to the Philosophers and well treated by them." *Guide*, 1:31. Compare al-Fārābī: "Most people have no ability, either by innate character or by custom, to understand and form a concept of [ideas in metaphysics and theology]. For those people, an image ought to be made, by means of which things that represent them, of how the principles, their rankings, the active intellect, and the first ruler come about." *Political Regime*, 74.

assumes his intended readers will be – will trace their authorship. They will ascribe them to Moses as a first ruler, and their purpose to his "kingly craft": Israel's religion.

As a first ruler, Moses draws on his faculty of imagination to render abstract philosophical insights accessible in religious terms and so bring his nation, step by step, to knowledge of God. This education begins with true beliefs. "If we did not receive some ideas somehow by faith," Maimonides explains, "rather than having to think purely conceptually ... everyone would die before learning even whether God exists."[149] Some of these beliefs, like God's "existence and unity, knowledge and power, will and eternity," state truths directly but do not justify them, appealing to authority rather than reason. Others are true only when understood metaphorically but are "critical to civic life": the "belief that God is filled with wrath toward those who flout His authority," or the corporeal resurrection of the dead.[150]

Some Straussian readers, noting the parallel between "necessary beliefs" and Plato's "noble lies," have argued that they are evidence for Maimonides' "Platonic politics."[151] Such beliefs do help sustain social order. Yet as Maimonides repeatedly stresses, their larger point is pedagogical: Over time, some will move past them to real knowledge.[152] Through the diligent pursuit of moral virtues and a curriculum of logic, mathematics, and the natural sciences, they will finally reach the study of theology.[153] They will understand bodily resurrection as metonymizing the intellect's immortality, reward and punishment as poeticizing God's general providence.[154] This achievement, granted, will not be reached by many. Yet as with al-Fārābī, this does not imply that the Torah's simulacrums of philosophy have a cynical aim. They are meant to educate and enlighten, not discipline and oppress, a point Maimonides hammers home by comparing their effect to nurturing children. To teach metaphysics to

---

[149] *Guide*, 1:34.

[150] "The Torah lays down certain beliefs critical to civic life – like the belief that God is filled with wrath toward those who flout His authority – to strike fear and consternation in the hearts of the fractious." *Guide*, 3:28. The material resurrection of the dead is not meant to be taken literally, but is instead a kind of symbolic representation of the rational soul's immortality, what al-Fārābī terms a "similitude" of the idea. As Maimonides makes clear elsewhere, the "world to come" is not a period of time but a state of being achieved after death by those who have sufficiently developed their minds while living. His *Treatise on Resurrection*, written in response to the accusation that he rejected a corporeal afterlife, was, in Joel Kraemer's words, a "masterful piece of rhetorical accommodation ... geared to the popular imagination." *Maimonides*, 418. It contained no substantive changes from his previously published views.

[151] Kraemer, *Maimonides*, 425. Indeed, Strauss referred to Maimonides' extensive discussions of the reasons for the commandments, as well as ethical virtue, as "long stretches of silence, i.e., of insignificant talk": sections to deflect the uninitiated or boorish reader from the *Guide's* subversive philosophical message. *Persecution*, 53–54.

[152] *Guide*, 1:50, 3:27–28.   [153] *Guide*, 1:34, 3:51.   [154] *Guide*, 3:10; *Introduction to Chelek*.

the unprepared, he writes, "seems no different from feeding meat and bread to a nursling, or giving him wine to drink. That would kill him, of course. . . . Just so, these true beliefs were veiled . . . not because they harbor some deep seated ill. . . . These themes were introduced obliquely because a mind cannot absorb them right from the start."[155]

Maimonides' more important debt to Plato, therefore, is arguably the distinction in the *Meno* between knowledge and belief.[156] For most people most of the time, true beliefs work as well as knowledge. Israel's teachers and leaders, however, need sound explanations rooted in philosophy. This is what motivated Rav Ashi's decision to include *derashot* in the Talmud, as we have seen. It is also what informed Moses' choice to begin the Torah with the Account of Creation [*Ma'aseh Bereshit*]:

> God, you see, chose to improve us and enhance our lives in society with His practical norms. But this could not be done without our attaining certain intellectual convictions – chiefly, an awareness of Him, so far as we are able. That depends on metaphysics, theological knowledge, which is won only after study of natural science. . . . That is why God opens His book with the Account of Creation, which belongs to physics.[157]

Maimonides again mutes the attribution, but those who have seen the *Guide* through to its end are positioned to understand its meaning. Moses was a philosopher who gained theoretical knowledge of God. But like a true philosopher in al-Fārābī's sense, this knowledge did not remain confined to itself. It manifested in *action*: laws which "improve us and enhance our lives in society." In the *Mishnah Commentary*, these are assembled in the Mishnah and codified in the Talmud. In the *Guide*, they are written in the Torah.

To assemble Israel's religion, Moses also draws upon a second of al-Fārābī's virtues: prudence or the "deliberative virtue," the ability to shape philosophy's universal findings to the mold of a particular people. A first ruler's fundamental aim is to grow his people's knowledge. Yet what will be required to effect this aim will differ widely based on time and place. Varied circumstances yield varied obstacles; different nations manifest different characteristics. In the Torah's context, Maimonides contends, the most important challenge Israel faced was religious: the temptation to idolatry. Idolatry is certainly a grave moral problem, and Maimonides highlights its depraved practices.[158] But it is also an epistemological one: By imagining a world of multiple gods and demonic forces, it turns people away from fundamental truths in physics,

---

[155] *Guide*, 1:33.

[156] Plato, *Meno and Phaedo*, ed. David Sedley, trans. Alex Long (New York: Cambridge University Press, 2010), 97a–b.

[157] *Guide*, 1: Introduction.   [158] *Guide*, 3:37.

metaphysics, and theology.[159] It derails religion's eidetic purpose. A major task of Moses' kingly craft, therefore, was to "free us from those sick ideas" and eliminate the idolatrous practices which sustain them: "The core of our entire Torah and the axis on which it turns is to erase such notions from the mind and efface all trace of them in the world."[160]

Yet in accomplishing this task, Moses had to confront an additional challenge: the distinctive qualities and experiences of Israel itself. A people born in slavery and accustomed to Egyptian polytheism could not be made, overnight, into a nation of philosophers. So, Moses settled for the next best alternative: He "preserved these ways of worship" – a *cultus* centered on sacrifices – "but shifted them to His name rather than objects manmade or imagined." Sacrifice, in other words, was retained as a concession to Israel's religious infancy. Spoken prayer is better; silent meditation is best of all. But just as God does not miraculously change the order of nature, He "does not use miracles to change human nature."[161]

Maimonides historicization of the sacrifices is well-known, and was one of the *Guide*'s most controversial arguments. Yet he also makes another, subtler point concerning the sacrifices which, while less frequently observed, is in many ways more revealing:

> Text and tradition agree that the earliest laws we received said nothing of sacrifices and burnt offerings. . . . Our sound tradition specifies, "Shabbat and civil laws were ordained at Marah" (B. Shabbat 87b, Sanhedrin 56b). Shabbat was the statute; the rule was civil law, against wrongdoing. The prime object, as I explained, was our holding true beliefs – belief in the world's creation. . . . Our first laws, you can see then, said nothing of sacrifices and burnt offerings. Those were secondary.[162]

Maimonides here is quietly advancing a radical claim. Not only was the written Torah revealed only gradually, at different points along the Sinai journey. The *content* of its revelation was shaped by its contingent history.[163] Originally, Moses wrote the Torah's civil laws and instituted Shabbat. The former framed the social order, while the latter supplied true beliefs – God's ex nihilo creation and ongoing providence. Only once the people showed their incapacity for unadorned monotheism was a sacrificial cult finally instituted. These laws were "secondary."

---

[159] *Guide*, 3:45.   [160] *Guide*, 3:29, 3:37.   [161] *Guide*, 3:32.   [162] *Guide*, 3:32.

[163] Maimonides makes a similar point about Yom Kippur. The day, despite its gravity, was not part of God's cosmological design or preordained by a "primordial" Torah, but originated in an event: Moses' descent from Sinai with the second set of tablets, bearing the message that Israel's sins had been forgiven. Indeed, each of the holidays can be understood as developed by Moses, using his prudence and imagination, to cultivate particular ideas (e.g. God's providence, the truth of prophecy) and virtues (e.g. humility and gratitude). *Guide*, 3:43.

Like Judah the Prince with the Mishnah or Rav Ashi with the Talmud, Moses attuned his text to his people's needs. He used his imagination to embed philosophical truths in its stories.[164] He applied his prudence to tailor its laws to its time and place. By virtue of his angelic intellect, God "created the words"; but the Law was written "in his own hand."[165] He was Israel's founding first ruler. The Torah was his kingly craft.

7 "Love Depends on Knowing": Imitating God

Handed only what we have seen, readers of the *Guide* might conclude that Israel could never produce another great leader. Moses is a singular, incomparable figure – an angel. How could anyone set out to be one of the intellects? Consequently, many interpreters have understood Maimonides as championing the contemplative life. For Strauss and like-minded commentators, the *Guide* is a coded message sent from one philosophical mountaintop to another. Others, while not necessarily sharing Strauss' views, have still seen it as following Arabic Neoplatonists like Ibn Bājjah in elevating thought over deed.[166] There have been some who read the text as making space for action.[167] Yet they have often limited this to a rarified few – the prophets, patriarchs, and Moses – and identified it, following al-Fārābī, with politics and legislation.[168] I believe Maimonides' theocratic aims point in a different direction. We should all strive for maximal knowledge of God. We should all try to obtain individual providence. But the status attained by Moses – a fully actualized intellect – is not a prerequisite for action; it is a regulative idea. Anyone whose knowledge of

---

[164] It should be emphasized, however, that according to Maimonides, the Mosaic revelation, in contrast to lesser instances of prophecy, did not involve the imagination, but was purely noetic. The function of Moses' imagination was to *translate* philosophy's insights into popularly accessible forms. See note 132. For an extended analysis, see Jeffrey Macy, "Prophecy in al-Farabi and Maimonides: The Imaginative and Rational Faculties," in *Maimonides and Philosophy*, ed. Shlomo Pines and Yirmiyahu Yovel (Dordrecht: Nijhoff, 1986).

[165] *Guide*, 1:2; "Hakdama [Introduction]," in *Mishneh Torah*, edited by Zvi H. Preisler (Jerusalem: Ketuvim [1180] 1993), 1:2.

[166] Alexander Altmann, "Maimonides' Four Perfections," *Israel Oriental Studies* 2 (1972): 169–70; Stephen Harvey, "Maimonides in the Sultan's Palace," in *Perspectives on Maimonides*, ed. Joel L. Kraemer (New York: Oxford University Press, 1991); "The Place of the Philosopher in the City according to Ibn Bajja," in *Political Aspects of Islamic Philosophy*, ed. Charles E. Butterworth (Cambridge: Harvard University Press, 1992); Kreisel, *Maimonides' Political Thought*.

[167] See for example Lawrence V. Berman, "Maimonides on Political Leadership," in *Kinship and Consent: The Jewish Political Tradition and Its Contemporary Uses*, ed. Daniel Elazar (Philadelphia: Turtledove, 1981).

[168] Berman, "Maimonides, the Disciple of Alfarabi," 26–48; Blidstein, `Ekronot mediniyim be-mishnat ha-Rambam`; Davidson, "Maimonides' Shemonah Peraqim and Alfarabi's Fusul al-Madani"; Miriam Galston, "Philosopher-King vs. Prophet," *Israel Oriental Studies* 88 (1978); Melamed, *Philosopher-King*.

God inspires love of God will seek to emulate God. And what we imitate about God, above all, are His attributes involved in rule.[169]

The link Maimonides forges between imitation and divine governance is grounded in two key psychological claims, the first being that knowledge of God leads to love of God. One might assume the opposite: Doesn't studying something require that I care about it first? Yet the kind of love people often associate with piety, Maimonides argues, is not really love. It misapprehends its object: To love God without first knowing Him is, at best, to love the bare outline drawn by true beliefs; at worst, it is to love a version of God who does not exist – one who has a body, emotions, or positive attributes.[170] "Love," he writes, in a chapter which he calls the "seal" of the *Guide*, "depends on knowing."[171] It is what the Sages call "worship of the heart," where heart, properly understood, means mind.[172] Maimonides acknowledges that such love is rare. Most people serve God out of fear of punishment or promise of reward.[173] But he also makes clear that it is not limited to sui generis figures like Abraham and Moses. In the *Mishneh Torah*'s commandment list, loving God comes third, following on the first, knowing God.[174] And Maimonides later expounds upon it in universal, not elitist terms: "One only loves God with the knowledge with which one knows Him. ... A person ought therefore to devote himself to the understanding and comprehension of those sciences and studies which will inform him concerning his Master."[175]

Maimonides' second psychological claim is that people emulate what they love; true love of God, therefore, inspires *imitatio dei*. In Plato's *Theaetetus*, imitating the divine is framed as a duty: We should strive to become as like to God as we can.[176] Maimonides, too, sometimes uses this language of obligation.

---

[169] As Peter Gordon observes, eros (*'ishq*, "passionate love") in Maimonides is not merely sexual love, but "more expansive," a "symbolic that pervades every sphere of life, the libidinal stuff out of which culture itself is formed." "The Erotics of Negative Theology: Maimonides on Apprehension," *Jewish Studies Quarterly* 2 (1995): 7. Compare al-Fārābī: "The first [cause], then ... is the primary beloved and the primary object of passion." *Political Regime*, 46. See also 64. I discuss the creative dimensions of Maimonidean love below. For the centrality of *imitatio dei* in Jewish thought more generally, see Lenn E. Goodman, *Love Thy Neighbor as Thyself* (New York: Oxford University Press, 2008).

[170] Maimonides refers to someone who assigns God positive predicates as an "unwitting atheist": The being this person refers to using the signifier "God" bears no relation what God actually is. *Guide*, 1:60.

[171] *Guide*, 3:51.

[172] Talmud Bavli, Tractate Ta'anit, 2a; Maimonides, *Introduction to Pirkei Avot [Ethics of the Fathers]*; *Hilchot Yesodei haTorah*, 2:2; *Guide*, 1:39, 3:28, 3:51.

[173] *Introduction to Chelek*; *Guide*, 3:17, 3:23, 3:29–30, 3:39, 3:53.

[174] Moses Maimonides, "Mitzvot Aseh [Positive Commandments]," in *Mishneh Torah*, ed. by Zvi H. Preisler. (Jerusalem: Ketuvim, [1180] 1993). §3.

[175] *Hilchot Teshuva*, 10:6.

[176] Plato, *Theaetetus and Sophist*, trans. Christopher Rowe (New York: Cambridge University Press, 2015), 176b.

"One who governs a state," he writes, "must emulate His 'attributes' to ensure that his actions as a leader are appropriate."[177] Elsewhere, however, he describes imitating God as a natural outgrowth of love. If God is a being "from whom good ever flows," a person will want to be such a being too.[178] Yet as many readers have pointed out, imitating God seems paradoxical for Maimonides. The *Guide*'s core theological lesson is that God's essence is unknowable, separated from human cognition by an unbridgeable chasm. What is there to imitate?

The answer, for Maimonides, are God's attributes of *action*. God exercises His general providence through nature. As a person delves deeper into nature's logic, therefore, he earns more insight into divine wisdom.[179] He discovers that the cosmological order is good: Ills mostly result from our own free choices – starting wars, oppressing neighbors, drinking to excess.[180] Where they do come from nature, they are part of the cycle of creation and destruction which gives rise to life itself, in the way a forest fire clears the ground for new shoots.[181] From nature's general course we can then cull more specific features to imitate:

> God's ways and "attributes," you can see, are one and the same: the acts that issue from Him in the world. Whenever an act of His is recognized, the trait expressed in such an act is predicated of Him, and He is assigned a corresponding epithet. For example, His care in guiding the development of animal embryos is recognized, how He fosters their powers and those of the ones that rear them, to protect the young from death and injury, preserve them from harm, and help them meet their needs. ... That is what 'mercy' means. So He is called merciful.[182]

Even so, an important issue remains. How can God's attributes be recognized as such? Nature, after all, is filled within innumerable "acts." Ewes nurture their newborns; but hawks carry off lambs for dinner. Both are equally natural. Which of the two should we imitate?

Maimonides responds by citing the Torah: "Moses saw *all His good*, all His works, but Scripture confines itself to these thirteen 'attributes,' since they reflect the acts by which He governs humankind."[183] The Torah itself, in other words, specifies those elements of God's general providence which we

---

[177] *Guide*, 1:54.   [178] *Guide*, 2:4, 2:37. See Kreisel, *Maimonides' Political Thought*, 130–36.

[179] *Guide*, 1:34, 1:38, 1:52–54, 3:51.   [180] *Guide*, 3:12.

[181] *Guide*, 1:69, 3:10–12, 3:22. For Maimonides, God's goodness can be reconciled with the (apparent) existence of evil by looking upon nature not as a series of particular occurrences – deaths, injustices, and the like – but as a totality. See especially *Guide*, 3:10. Earlier in the *Guide* Maimonides had analogized this dynamic of divine providence to the circulations of the human body: "Just as the same forces that foster a human being's development and survival also compass his dissolution and decay, the causes of generation in the world at large are identical to those that bring decay." *Guide*, 1:72.

[182] *Guide*, 1:54.   [183] *Guide*, 1:54.

should emulate – the ones concerned with *rule*, or more generally, "those expressive of our good traits and dispositions."[184] It was precisely how "[God] governs humankind," Maimonides writes, which "was the ultimate object of Moses' request. Hence his closing words: *and know Thee, that I may find favor in Thine eyes. For this nation is Thy people* (Exodus 33:13) – whom I must govern, by modeling my ways on Yours."[185]

Still, that cannot be the full story. Moses, as we have seen, was a true philosopher in al-Fārābī's sense – a first ruler. He arrived at theoretical knowledge of God. The attributes he assigned to God in the Torah were thus derived, presumably, from this knowledge. They had a basis in not merely in tradition but philosophy. Yet even if philosophy is universal, it is not uniform. Unlike the findings of mathematics, those of philosophy and theology are the shakiest and most generative of controversy.[186] So it is not enough to say that Moses found God through reason.[187] We have to ask: *Which* God? Who was the deity philosopher Moses discovered and whose rule he sought to imitate?

One might assume that Maimonides' Moses shares his God with al-Fārābī. Not only did al-Fārābī provide the template for Maimonides' theocratic project, as we have seen; he makes *imitatio dei* central to defining the first ruler's place and functions. Al-Fārābī develops his account of divine imitation from the *Timaeus*, what he calls Plato's book on "Lordship" [*al-rububiyya*].[188] Plato here presents the human mind as a kind of microcosm emulating the macrocosm:

> For the divine element in us, the motions which are akin to it are the thoughts and revolutions of the whole world. Everyone should take a lead from these. We should correct the corrupted revolutions in our head concerned with becoming (*genesis*), by learning the harmonies and revolutions of the whole world, and so make the thinking subject resemble the object of its thought, in accordance with its ancient nature; and, by creating this resemblance, bring to fulfillment (*telos*) the best life offered by the gods to mankind for present and future time.[189]

Becoming godlike, in the *Timaeus*, means emulating the divine cosmology. Like the spheres, our minds should be self-sufficient. Our thoughts should be intellectual. Our motions should be volitionless and eternal, propelled not by will but cosmic harmony. Al-Fārābī portrays the first ruler's *imitatio dei* in very similar terms:

> When the ruler, after making these rankings [of rulership among his subjects], then wants to define a command . . . he intimates that to the rankings closest to him; and they intimate it to whoever comes after them. Then it goes on like

---

[184] *Guide*, 1:60.   [185] *Guide*, 1:54.   [186] *Guide*, 1:31.   [187] *Guide*, 1:63.
[188] *Harmonization*, 156–57.
[189] Translation from David Sedley, "Becoming Godlike," in *The Cambridge Companion to Ancient Ethics*, ed. Christopher Bobonich (New York: Cambridge University Press, 2017), 326.

that until it arrives at the one who is ranked as serving that affair. Thus the parts of the city are then tied to one another. . . . It comes to resemble the natural existents, and its rankings also resemble the rankings of the existents that begin at the first [cause] and terminate at primary material and the elements. . . . And the governor of that city is similar to the first cause through which the rest of the existents exist.[190]

In al-Fārābī's description, the first ruler is a distant, almost passive figure. Like the First Cause, he sustains the regime through ideas sent down the ranks of a political order whose harmony closely mirrors that of the cosmos. He does not will; he emanates. He does not command; he "intimates." He impinges on the world in a purely delegated way.[191]

Maimonides' Moses, by contrast, is a kind of theological voluntarist.[192] He sees the world as created ex nihilo, and only afterward arranged into the delegated harmony of intellects, spheres, and human beings.[193] His God "willed the world to be that once did not exist but now has come to be, by His will."[194] And it is this

---

[190] *Political Regime*, 73.

[191] There is in fact some ambiguity as to whether al-Fārābī's perfected ("happy") human being affects the world at all. While the passage just cited suggests that he does, elsewhere al-Fārābī strongly implies that once a soul achieves the rank of the Active Intellect it disconnects entirely from its material surroundings: "When [the rational part of the soul] becomes completely separated from all the parts of the soul apart from it, its existence also comes to be limited to itself alone and does not emanate to anything apart from it." *Political Regime*, 39.

[192] Although Maimonides had argued in his *Mishnah Commentary* that the world was created for man's sake, his position in the *Guide* is that God's purpose in creation is unknowable and must be ascribed to His volition alone. *Guide*, 3:13. See also 2:11. Once created, however, the world is eminently receptive to rational explanation in terms of its regular laws and cycles. Likewise the Torah's laws, which, Maimonides insists against the voluntarists, express not "His sheer will," but "have reasons and were given to afford some benefit." *Guide*, 3:26. See also 3:31, 3:49.

[193] *Guide*, 2:16–22. Maimonides' position on the world's creation or eternality is the subject of significant scholarly debate. In brief, some have argued that Maimonides sees creation as a "necessary belief," a mask for his true fidelity to Aristotle or *formatio mundi*. Herbert Davidson, "Maimonides' Secret Position on Creation," in *Studies in Medieval Jewish History and Literature*, ed. Isadore Twersky (Cambridge: Harvard University Press, 1979); Fraenkel, *Philosophical Religions*; Strauss, *Philosophy and Law*. Maimonides is indeed modest about what philosophy can show in this area; neither eternality nor creation is rationally demonstrable. *Guide*, 2:16. But he also thinks there are good reasons to support creation. And he contends that these are the same reasons which can be found in the "Torah of our Teacher Moses." *Introduction to Chelek*; *Guide*, 2:13, 2:28. Likewise, while Maimonides does argue that God governs the universe via emanation, he stresses, in contrast to Neoplatonists like Plotinus, that God does not emanate by *necessity*, but – at least in the initial act of creation – by *will*: "We then recognize that this Being, whose essence is His existence, suffices not only to its own being but also to shed being on many things more, not as heat flows from a flame, or light is entailed by the sun, of necessity, but in a flow ever sustaining and wisely ordering and governing the rest." *Guide*, 1:58. See also 1:69.

[194] *Guide*, 2:21. "We meet Aristotle half way: We believe the world will last forever and will always have the nature God was pleased to give it, quite unchanged, unless miraculously in some particular (although God has the power to change it wholly, to annihilate it, or to void any nature He pleases). But the world did begin." *Guide*, 2:29. As Maimonides elaborates, the danger of eternalism is twofold. First, by turning God into a kind of mechanism without will, and so

willing and creating deity which he renders, through his kingly craft, into the Torah's model for emulation.[195] Plato's portrait of divine mimesis in the *Timaeus* neither demands nor implies anything from us morally. How we treat other people – or indeed, how we interact with the physical world itself – is entirely derivative. Everything, quite literally, takes place inside our heads. Moses' God, by contrast, does not dwell at the heights of heaven. He is actively involved in the world: sewing clothes for Adam and Eve, raining fire on Sodom and Gomorrah, and providing Abraham and Sarah with a son in their old age.[196] True, many of the Torah's narratives are not, for Maimonides, meant to be taken literally. Yet neither are they noble lies. They are religious translations of philosophical ideas: God really *could* intervene in the world as a manifestation of his Goodness.[197] So, by extension, should we.

8 "The Human Attainment Rightly Gloried in Is Ruling Them as He Does": Rule of God, Rule of the Good

Al-Fārābī, an eternalist, limits *imitatio dei* to the first ruler, the human embodiment of Aristotle's First Cause. While the first ruler does delegate his rule, ultimately "God's governance in another way" is his responsibility. Everyone else obeys him. Maimonides, by contrast, broadens *imitatio dei* to anyone who

---

rendering miracles impossible, it undermines the authority of the law bolstered by promises of reward and threats of punishment. Second, by rendering all things determined, it undermines human freedom, without which we cannot be assigned responsibility for following or abnegating God's laws (and which, in turn, makes God unjust for commanding them).

[195] For al-Fārābī, by contrast, religion emulates not God's attributes of action, but the "intelligibles" which make up the divine cosmology: "[Religion] imitates the actions of natural powers and principles by their likenesses among the faculties, states, and arts that have to do with the will, just as Plato does in the Timaeus." *Attainment of Happiness*, 77. Elsewhere al-Fārābī reads the *Timaeus* as a continuation of the *Republic*, arguing that Plato's cosmological account plays a practical role in Callipolis by providing a model for its citizens to emulate. *Philosophy of Plato*, 65–66.

[196] Maimonides likewise stresses divine volition in his discussion of prophecy. He argues that there are three views of prophecy, each of which corresponds to a stance on the world's creation or eternality. The first, rooted in a kind of occasionalist voluntarism, regards prophecy as a matter of pure divine decision. In the same way that God is constantly recreating every atom in the universe, He can also decide to make any person (or animal) receive prophecy at will, without any qualifications. A second view, which Maimonides associates with the philosophers' eternalist naturalism, is that prophecy is a purely human attainment. If a person has the requisite moral and intellectual qualifications, he cannot but prophesize. The final view Maimonides associates with the Torah, combining voluntarism with a belief in nature's constancy once being created. Like the philosophers, the Torah regards a person's virtues as necessary for prophecy; unlike them, it does not see them as sufficient. God must still *will* this person to be a prophet: "We hold that someone fit for prophecy and suitably prepared might fail to prophesy, by God's will." *Guide*, 2:32. Here is a kind of mirror image of Maimonides' sophisticated view of creation: Divine volition yields a fixed natural order; within this order, God may then choose to intervene.

[197] *Guide*, 3:32.

genuinely knows and loves God. He does this by carving out a space for divine will: In practice, the natural order is "fixed"; in principle, God could use the same power with which He created the universe to miraculously overturn any aspect of it. It is this principle of divine volition which the Torah's stories and homilies convey. And it is this principle – not the practice of God's restraint and mediation – which underlies our *imitatio dei*. Maimonides does not democratize divine rule in the way Martin Buber later would.[198] True "worship of the heart" is rare. But he does open it up to anyone who diligently pursues wisdom. By emulating qualities attributed to God's Goodness – justice (*mishpat*), righteousness (*tzedakah*), and kindness (*chesed*) – we become, in effect, worldly agents of the voluntarism God opts not to express.[199] And through us, the rule of God, Maimonides' theocratic project, takes on a distinctive form: rule of the Good.[200]

Maimonides confronts al-Fārābī's view in the midst of a series of chapters on Aristotle's eternalism. Al-Fārābī, Maimonides argues, believed the world's permanence was proven, and ridiculed those, like Galen, who considered the issue unresolved.[201] This certainty, in turn, shaped al-Fārābī's understanding of prophecy. Prophecy posed a key challenge for Muslim and Jewish Neoplatonists: How can God limit revelation? If prophesizing is identical to attaining the Active Intellect, shouldn't it be possible, in principle, for anyone? Al-Fārābī agrees. The only thing which holds back prophecy is the disposition, knowledge, and training of the potential prophet.[202] Maimonides takes a different position. Citing al-Fārābī's *On the Intellect*, he notes that his predecessor is "clearly right" about the Active Intellect. Where he and all eternalists err is in making the same inferences about God. Ultimately, divine will and wisdom are one and the same; reasons underly all created things. From our limited perspective, however, many elements in the universe, like the precise

---

[198] For more on Buber's concept of theocracy – what he calls "theopolitics" – see my article "Theopolitics Contra Political Theology."

[199] *Mishpat* is defined by Maimonides as "legal justice, giving those judged the reward or retribution they deserve." *Tzedakah* is also a kind of justice, but one practiced out of one's own moral qualities and desire to do good for its own sake, not on the basis of contractual obligations or fear of punishment. It is "what virtue demands in your treatment of others." *Chesed*, often translated as "kindness," "lovingkindness," or "grace," is "benefiting someone who has no claim on one or helping someone who has a claim but giving more than is deserved." In this sense, the whole world is a manifestation of divine *chesed*, an "overflow" of divine goodness neither requested nor earned. Maimonides explains how each of these qualities might be ascribed to God: "As Creator of the universe he is called kind. For His mercy toward the helpless, governing all living beings through their natural powers, He is called righteous. And for the relative good and ills, and the cosmic disasters mandated by His wisdom and justice, He is called Judge." *Guide*, 3:53.

[200] For more on the identification of God with His goodness, including in Maimonides, see Lenn E. Goodman, *The Holy One of Israel* (Oxford: Oxford University Press, 2019), especially ch. 2.

[201] *Guide*, 2:15.

[202] *Attainment of Happiness*, 76–81; *Religion*, 94, 97–98; *Political Regime*, 48–49, 69.

location of the stars, seem arbitrary, so we assign them to God's will. The same goes for prophecy: God can withhold it at his will.[203]

Maimonides' defense of divine volition holds important lessons for *imitatio dei* as well. The God of al-Fārābī (and Aristotle) might "stand at the highest, most perfect rank of being." But He cannot be said to have a "purpose" in His creation. Emulating such a God, by extension, means cauterizing our volition. It means affirming the world as it is: "Notions of intending and determining apply only to what does not yet exist but might or might not, depending on what is determined by the purpose of a subject."[204] Indeed for al-Fārābī, the achievement of happiness, in its highest form, requires leaving this flawed world behind. It comes only in dying.[205] The Torah of Moses, by contrast, is about what we can do in life – for ourselves, and for the sake of heaven. In his *Mishnah Commentary*, Maimonides had conveyed this idea by reinterpreting the Talmudic saying: "The Holy One has in His World Only the Four Cubits of the Law." In the *Guide*, he subtly inverts this aphorism to communicate the same message:

> Of all things celestial, man has just this modicum of mathematics. . . . As the Torah puts it lyrically, *"The heavens are the heavens of the Lord, but the earth He gave to the sons of man* (Psalms 115:16). . . . [God] gave mankind the power to know the world below. It is our world. We are placed here and belong here.[206]

The earth is not just an antechamber. Human beings should not just passively accept the world's injustices, study philosophy, and wait for death. We have a higher purpose.

Maimonides seals the link between *imitatio dei* and divine rule in the *Guide*'s concluding chapter. In the pages just prior, he had reiterated that knowledge of God should be our supreme aim. We should strive for the "intellectual virtues," not fleeting pursuits like "wealth, health, and character," a point about which the philosophers and prophets agree: "Thus saith the Lord, 'Let not the wise man glory in his might nor the rich man in his wealth, but let him who would glory glory in this: that he understandeth and knoweth me*" (Jeremiah: 22–23).[207]

---

[203] *Guide*, 2:18, 2:36.   [204] *Guide*, 2:20.

[205] "On the Intellect," in *Classical Arabic Philosophy: An Anthology of Sources* (Indianapolis: Hackett: 2007), 76; *Harmonization*, 164–65; *Political Regime*, 48–49. As al-Fārābī writes in *Religion*: "[True happiness] does not come about in this life, but rather in the next life which is after this one." *Religion*, 101. Elsewhere he describes this process transpiring on a collective level – and indeed, as one of the aims of just rulership: "When a group passes away, their bodies are nullified, and their souls are delivered and made happy, then other people follow after them, take their place in the city, and perform their activities; the souls of these [people], too, are delivered. When their bodies are nullified, they come to the rankings of those in this group who have passed away. . . . This, then, is the true happiness that is the purpose of the active intellect." *Political Regime*, 71–72.

[206] *Guide*, 2:24.   [207] *Guide*, 3:54.

Maimonides' elevation of theoretical knowledge has led some readers to argue that his final position, in the *Guide*, favors the contemplative life. This is understandable: Maimonides does define all other pursuits as means to wisdom. While the Torah's "acts of piety and morality" are highly valuable, they "hold not a candle to this ultimate goal." By the end of the chapter, however, this seems to shift. Maimonides returns to the verse from Jeremiah and completes it: "Jeremiah does not stop at naming our highest goal, knowledge of God. . . . The verse specifies the actions we must know and emulate: kindness, justice, and righteousness (*chesed, mishpat,* and *tzedakah*)." This turn has long occupied Maimonides' interpreters: Is it a "strange" shift in perspective?[208] A rhetorical device to deceive nonphilosophers?[209] A return from the fields of philosophy back to the thickets of *halacha*?[210]

What we have seen of Maimonides' theocratic project suggests an alternative reading. Knowledge is indeed our ultimate end. But knowledge, as we have seen, is neither inert nor idle. It begets *action*. To be a true philosopher, for al-Fārābī, is also to be a first ruler. To be a "complete" man, we saw in the *Mishnah Commentary*, means "mind" and "deed," being "wise" and "good." Such were men like Judah the Prince and Rav Ashi. And as we learn in the *Guide*, so too was Moses. Yet what, in practice, does such agency entail? If we can't be first rulers like Moses, can we still advance God's governance? Al-Fārābī said no. If a true philosopher's stature is not recognized by his people, "the fact that he is of no use to others is not his fault."[211] Let the world continue as it may – the philosopher should withdraw, devote himself to contemplation, tend his own garden.

Maimonides, by contrast, believes God's rulership is a project open, in principle, to all. The Mosaic legislation is immutable; but "every human being may become righteous like Moses."[212] He explains how in concluding the *Guide*, reflecting on Jeremiah:

> Contrary to what the rash pretend, who suppose God's care stops at the sphere of the moon and slights the earth. . . . Providence, Jeremiah says, cares for the earth too, as befits it, just as it cares for the heavens as befits them. . . . What the verse means, then, is that the human attainment rightly gloried in, clearly, is to reach, so far as one can, an awareness of God and His care for His creatures, giving them being and ruling them as He does. One who wins such awareness will ever show kindness, justice, and righteousness in life, emulating God's acts.[213]

The God of Israel is not the First Cause of Aristotle. He has not abandoned us to our fate. His providence guides both heaven and earth. But He rules over each

---

[208] Guttmann, *Dat u-madda.*   [209] Strauss, "Remarks."
[210] Soloveitchik, *Maimonides: Between Philosophy and Halakhah*; Yeshaiahu Leibowitz, *The Faith of Maimonides*, trans. John Glucker (New York: Adama, 1987).
[211] *Attainment of Happiness*, 81.   [212] *Hilchot Teshuva*, 5:2.   [213] *Guide*, 3:54.

domain according to what "befits it." For the intellects and spheres, it is assured. For human beings, God's governance proceeds by "another way": through us. What God showed Moses, in the chapter Maimonides refers to here, was "His Good" (Exodus 33:19) – the goodness inherent in God's general providence, and the goodness by which God exercises providence on earth.[214] What is this latter goodness? *Our* actions in imitating him. The cosmological order cannot but be good. We, by contrast, have to *make* this world good by acting with the attributes the Torah assigns to God: justice, righteousness, and kindness. We know God, love God, and emulate God. We give "being" to the world and "rule" over it just as He does.

And this is not only a task for high politics. True, there is a sense in which divine mimesis, for Maimonides, is a "political *imitatio dei*": This is what emulating God looked like for Moses.[215] But we should not allow the idiom of "rule" to limit what is in fact a far broader concept. Knowledge of God cannot be switched on or off based on context. It is something a person carries wherever he goes, a "great majesty who is always with him and in touch with him, greater than any human king."[216] And such awareness, through love, transforms even his most mundane acts. Moses and the Patriarchs could be "engaged as leaders, or in acquiring property," while "their minds never left His presence."[217] Some have interpreted Maimonides here to suggest a kind of existential dualism: The greatness of these men was that they could philosophize even while stooping to baser matters.[218] This might accord with Ibn Tufayl, Plotinus, or Plato. Yet Maimonides, in concluding the passage, points us in a different direction: "The aim of their efforts, lifelong, was to found a nation that knew and served God."[219] By infusing all of their actions, from the profound to quotidian, with knowledge and love of God, Moses and the Patriarchs turned every activity, every moment, into an opportunity to imitate God. They engaged with the world *because* of their wisdom, not in spite of it. They sought to manifest goodness and inspire others to do the same.[220] Contra Strauss, then, Moses was not

---

[214] *Guide*, 3:54.

[215] Lawrence V. Berman, "The Political Interpretation of the Maxim: The Purpose of Philosophy is the Imitation of God," *Studia Islamica* 15 (1961); Harvey, "Bein filosofiyah medinit le-halakhah be-mishnat ha-Rambam."; Kreisel, *Maimonides' Political Thought*, ch. 4; Steven Schwarzschild, "Moral Radicalism and 'Middlingness' in the Ethics of Maimonides," *Studies in Medieval Culture* 11 (1977).

[216] *Guide*, 3:52. Earlier in the *Guide*, Maimonides had analogized reason's function in human self-organization to God's rulership over the universe. *Guide*, 1:72.

[217] *Guide*, 3:51.   [218] See for example Ravitzky, *Philosophy and Leadership in Maimonides*.

[219] *Guide*, 3:51.

[220] The idea that knowledge of God can be sustained in the midst of worldly action contrasts sharply with al-Fārābī: "Sometimes I am alone with my soul a great deal and I cast off my body and become like an abstract, incorporeal substance … I am at one and the same time knowledge, the knower, and the known. … When I am immersed in that light, reach my

a Schmittian tyrant imposing his arbitrary will on a beguiled people. He was just the opposite: an instrument of God's rule – an agent for the Good.[221]

Maimonides begins the *Guide* by invoking the same passage from Avot, which he had linked, in his *Mishnah Commentary*, to humanity's role in realizing divine rule: "Let all your deeds be for the sake of heaven."[222] He concludes it with two passages from Isaiah, the first of which reads: "Then shall the eyes of the blind be opened and the ears of the deaf be unstopped (Isaiah 35:5)."[223] Taken in isolation, this verse is about knowledge for its own sake. But in context – one Maimonides surely expects us to know – it is about redemption: "Say to the anxious of heart, / 'Be strong, fear not; / Behold your God! / Requital is coming, / The recompense of God – He Himself is coming to give you triumph.'"[224] We are now positioned to postulate about its meaning. Through reason, our minds can access the same divine emanation which flows through the order of nature. And when this flow is strong enough – when we attain the Active Intellect – our actions *become* God's actions. We transform into agents of providence; knowledge turns into rule. Maimonides then adds one more quote from Isaiah: "The nation that walked in darkness shall see a great light. On those who live in the land of deep gloom a light shall dawn!" (9:1).[225] This, perhaps, was Maimonides' aim with the *Guide* itself: By restoring philosophy to its rightful place in Israel, he sought to restore Israel to its rightful place among the nations.

Coda: Democracy and the Rule of God

> Moses said to the Lord, "See, You say to me, 'Lead this people forward.'
> . . . Now, if I have truly gained Your favor, pray let me know Your ways, that
> I may know You and continue in Your favor. Consider, too, that this nation is Your
> people."
> . . . And [the Lord] answered, "I will make all My Good pass before you."
>
> *Exodus 33:12–13, 33:19*

I began this study with two questions derived from Jürgen Habermas: What has theocracy meant historically? What might it still mean today? I have offered an answer to the first by reconstructing Maimonides' theocratic project. For Maimonides, the heart of divine rule is the Neoplatonic idea of "emanation." God exercises general providence by imbuing the governing elements of the cosmos – the incorporeal intellects and heavenly spheres – with form. He effects

---

limit, and can no longer bear it, I descend to the world of calculation. When I arrive in the world of calculation, calculation conceals the light from me." *Harmonization*, 164–65.

[221] Strauss wrote his essays on the *Guide* and al-Fārābī in 1935–36, only shortly after his 1932 remarks on Schmitt's *Concept of the Political* and just prior to his 1936 book on Hobbes. This may help to explain why he imagined Moses as a kind of Schmittian sovereign.

[222] *Guide*, Advice about this Work.   [223] *Guide*, 3:54.   [224] Isaiah, 35:4.   [225] *Guide*, 3:54.

particular providence through us. When the human mind approaches the pinnacle of reason, our actions in essence become divine actions; in joining with the Active Intellect, we attach ourselves cognitively to God. Yet the upshot of this connection is not only noetic. Maimonides, I showed, follows al-Fārābī in arguing that one who has achieved such an intellectual level epitomizes both thought and leadership, "mind" and "deed." As a philosopher, he grasps truths in their pure rational form. As a legislator, he translates those truths into laws, morals, rituals, and beliefs. Thus contra Strauss, I argued that Maimonides' intention in the *Guide* was not "Platonic politics" – mass obedience for the sake of a philosophical elite. It was theocratic politics: an effort to realize the rule of God. The highest purpose of a leader is to guide his people – according to their particular history, context, and frailties – to genuine knowledge, or at least true beliefs, about the deity. In the divine division of labor, therefore, the "good" of the world depends on our moral and intellectual development. The goodness of nature is ineluctable, a pure manifestation of divine wisdom. The goodness of humanity is a product of the extent that we know, love, and imitate God. The more that we succeed, the more God can be said to rule.

What could theocracy mean today? Can Maimonides help us answer this question too? Theocracy, as I have referred to it here, refers not to priestly domination (hierocracy) but to how the divine being exercises sovereignty over the universe. This definition cannot aid the empirical study of religion and politics. Even so, I believe it has important normative implications. Are theocracy and democracy necessarily incompatible? Or can there be a place for the rule of God even within a democratic political order? These are the questions I will explore in concluding this study. And while I will not presume to answer them fully, I do think that Maimonides' approach may hold special relevance in our own time. Movements seeking to replace democracy with clerical rule claim to speak in God's name. Maimonides' thought, I believe, shows us one way we might respond. In extrapolating his ideas – albeit in ways he could not have anticipated, and might not have accepted – we find intriguing and neglected means by which elements of theocracy might coexist with, or even complement, democratic legitimacy.

Any attempt to associate Maimonides with democracy will strike many as far-fetched. Governance in his writings is nearly synonymous with kingship. Indeed while Aviezer Ravitzky identifies no less than four Maimonidean models of rule, each of these, from the "illegitimate sovereign" to the "ideal leader," is monarchical.[226] The Talmud debates whether kingship is mandated

---

[226] Ravitzky also notes a fifth model: a nonpolitical utopia which does not involve rule at all. *Religion and State in Jewish Philosophy*, 28–30.

by the Torah or merely optional. Maimonides unambiguously sides with the former view.[227] Moreover, normative political order in Maimonides is of a distinctively anti-modern type: the juridical unity of religion and state. Contemporary democracy rests on competitive elections and what Michael Walzer has called liberalism's "art of separation": within government, the division of powers; beyond it, the stratification of different layers of life (state, civil society, family) and spheres of value (politics, economics, ethics, aesthetics). Yet as Menachem Lorberbaum has shown, Maimonides – in contrast to certain later rabbinic figures – saw all of the polity's laws and institutions, civil and religious, as uniformly governed by *halacha* (Jewish law).[228] Finally, royalism plays a central role in Maimonides' messianism. Even as he drains the messianic age of supernatural elements and the messiah himself of miraculous powers, and even as he exhorts people not to focus on the fantastic events traditionally associated with its advent (such as the prophet Elijah's return), Maimonides stresses that the Messiah will be a "king ... from the house of David" who "re-establish[es] the monarchy."[229]

---

[227] "Rabbi Yehuda would say: 'Three *mitzvot* [commands] were commanded to the Jewish people upon entering the land of Israel: to establish a king for themselves [Deuteronomy 17:14–15], to cut off the seed of Amalek [Deuteronomy 25:17–19], and to build the Chosen House [i.e. the Temple] [Deuteronomy 12:10–12].' Rabbi Nehorai says, 'This [biblical] passage about appointing a king was stated only in response to [Israel's] complaint, as it is said, '[When you come unto the land that the Lord your God gives you, and shall possess it, and shall dwell therein,] and shall say: I will set a king over me [like all the nations that are around me] [Deuteronomy 17:14].'" Talmud Bavli, Tractate Sanhedrin: 20b. Maimonides follows Rabbi Yehuda's opinion and codifies the command to appoint a king in his *Mishneh Torah, Hilchot Melachim*, 1.1.

[228] See *Politics and the Limits of Law*. As Lorberbaum further shows, Maimonides' integralist approach can be contrasted with later figures, like Nissim Gerondi, who envisioned an autonomous domain for law and political action, prefiguring the West's secularized *raison d'état*.

[229] "A person must never busy himself with the tales (*Aggadah*) ... regarding these matters or similar issues. He must not turn them into dogma [*Ikarim*]." *Hilchot Melachim*, 12:2. Anticipating the *Guide*'s stress on the stability of nature, Maimonides in the *Mishneh Torah* insists that the messianic age will neither require nor bring about the overturning of natural laws. It will take place in the world we know. The lion will not literally lie down with the lamb. *Hilchot Melachim*, 12:1; *Guide*, 2:28–29. Human nature will likewise persist: While God could have changed our moral psychology to ensure unvarying obedience to *halacha*, "God does not use miracles to change human natures." *Guide*, 3:32. Thus unlike in many strands of Christian thought, redemption does not rely on any miraculous act of grace, for in Maimonides' account of the Tree of Knowledge, there is no stain of "original sin" to lustrate (see note 117). Finally, the messiah himself is a human being through and through. He performs no miracles and shows no wonderous "signs." He is an educator, creator, and field marshal: He teaches Torah to Israel, rebuilds the sanctuary, gathers the exiles, and "fights the Wars of God." He need not even be certain of his identity: Maimonides notes that if one sets out to accomplish these ends and fails to do so, he is not reprimanded, but rather considered "like all the exemplary and qualified kings of the House of David who have died." *Hilchot Melachim*, 11:5. While Maimonides' messianism is political and activist, Jewish messianism has historically taken a wide variety of forms, including those which stress ethical life rather than politics. For one example, see my "Against Politics: Walter Benjamin on Justice, Judaism, and the Possibility of Ethics," *American Political Science Review* 108, no. 1 (2014).

Maimonides' monarchism has likewise been a touchstone for certain strands of religious Zionism. Early thinkers associated with this movement confronted a dilemma. On the one hand, they sought to interpret the Zionist project and the state of Israel in messianic terms – the "first flowering of redemption" – or at the very least as legitimate forms of Jewish political expression. On the other hand, Israel is not a monarchy; it has no direct biblical or rabbinic analogue. How can such a state claim religious imprimatur? One response, as Alexander Kaye has shown, was not to abandon Maimonides' normative-legal requirement of kingship, but to reinterpret it. Maimonides describes the procedure for appointing kings as via a *Sanhedrin* (high court) of seventy elders accompanied by a prophet.[230] But as neither king nor *Sanhedrin* nor prophet were available in the twentieth century, some rabbinic figures sought to recast all three in democratic terms. Ideally, Jewish kings are elected by a consent of the majority. Only in circumstances where such consent is denied can the *Sanhedrin* override the people. And if political authority actually adheres foremost in the people, then references to "monarchy" in biblical and rabbinic texts need not be understood literally. They function as placeholders for all forms of government approved by popular consent, including democracy.[231]

This approach is undoubtedly innovative; yet aside from being a tendentious way to read Maimonides, it also remains deeply problematic from the perspective of democracy. First, monarchy is retained as a viable political option. While democratic institutions were chosen at Israel's founding, there is nothing to guarantee their permanence. The people – or someone claiming to speak in their name – may one day opt for something else. This leads to a second problem: "Democracy," as invoked here, bears only limited resemblance to the term's contemporary meaning. Modern liberal democracies restrain state power, protect individual rights from the majority, and hold regular elections. Popular consent is conceived as continuous process, not a single event. The form of democracy read into classical Jewish texts, by contrast, more closely tracks Thomas Hobbes' description of Leviathan's founding: a total transfer of sovereignty from a group of people to a king or counsel, with no retained rights or powers.[232] And this points to a final problem: This approach does not truly

---

[230] *Hilchot Melachim*, 1:3. After the initial coronation the monarchy becomes dynastic, though Maimonides argues (in line with his messianic thought) that only the Davidic line will be permanent. *Hilchot Melachim*, 1:7–9.

[231] This approach was associated especially with Rabbi Shaul Yisraeli. For an extended discussion, see Kaye, *The Invention of Jewish Theocracy*, ch. 6.

[232] *On the Citizen (De Cive)* (Cambridge: Cambridge University Press, [1642] 2003), 72–73. For an extended analysis of how we might read Hobbes as a kind of democratic theorist, see my article "Radical Democracy's Religion: Hobbes on Language, Domination, and Self-Creation," *Religions* 14, no. 11 (2023).

advocate for democracy, even in this limited Hobbesian form. Despite using the term "democracy" – rule of the "*demos*" or populace – neither the people nor their basic rights retain ultimate authority. *Halacha* reigns supreme. Whatever laws the people might institute, they are inevitably secondary to the Torah's laws. Political authority depends on religious authority, secular law on divine law. This religious Zionist view thus represents what John Rawls called a "*modus vivendi*" commitment to democracy: a temporary settlement to be replaced, when the time is ripe, with religious rule.[233]

In the remainder of these reflections, I will propose an alternative way we might draw upon Maimonides in relating democracy to divine rule. The religious Zionist view I noted grounds itself in Maimonidean jurisprudence: Because the *halacha* calls for monarchy, it assumes that Maimonides would mandate, if not kingship itself, then at least a conception of state power that accords with it. The hallmark of Jewish theocracy is thus a *halachic* state; God is sovereign when Jewish law reigns. I will not contest the authority Maimonides assigns to *halacha*. He makes plain not only the immutability of the written (Torah) law but the incontestable status of legislation derived from or instituted by the rabbinic sages.[234] What I will propose instead is a shift in emphasis. Maimonides, as we have seen, does not see law as humanity's highest aim. *Halacha* should be studied, revered, and followed. Yet in the last analysis it is not an end in itself, but rather a *means* for realizing greater ends: social order, individual discipline, moral virtue, and, ultimately, knowledge of God, manifesting in love and *imitatio dei* – our part in realizing divine rule. "Our ultimate goal in every context," Maimonides writes, in an especially direct expression of this idea in the *Guide*, "is to know God. . . . All those biblical practices – the acts of piety and morality so beneficial in our human interactions – hold not a candle to this ultimate goal but only pave the way to it."[235]

The question, then, is this: If we take Maimonides' teleological account of human life seriously – if everything we do in ethics, politics, and ordinary life should be directed toward acquiring divine wisdom – does realizing this *telos* actually require human kingship? Can our "ultimate goal" of knowing God be achieved without a *halachic* state? God, as we have seen, can be said to rule when we know Him. Can He rule just as well in a liberal democracy? I believe the answer is yes. If we consider Maimonides' political program in light of his teleology, it becomes possible to see how divine rule might be realized in a genuinely democratic context. Theocracy and democracy need not be adversaries. The former can exist – even thrive – within the latter.

---

[233] See "The Idea of Public Reason Revisited," 780–81.
[234] "Mitzvot Lo Ta'aseh," §§368–70.   [235] *Guide*, 3:54.

To be clear, I am not suggesting that this is an answer Maimonides himself would give. Maimonides lived out his whole life in the political and intellectual milieu of medieval Islam; he would recognize neither liberalism nor democracy as viable forms of political order.[236] More generally, it is impossible to speculate how a figure transported across vast developments in thought, culture, and politics would react to these changes. Yet neither, I think, should this keep us from asking the question. Ideas, while nurtured in a particular context, grow to take on their own identity. Maimonides continues to draw readers because his ideas continue to speak to us. They remain vital for thinking about our own lives and place in the world. And, after centuries of sitting quietly on the shelves of pious scholars and recondite philosophers, they have been brought out, loudly and prominently, into a new world of Jewish politics, acquiring renewed meaning, greater stakes, and practical urgency. What I aim to do here, therefore, is not claim to speak for Maimonides himself. It is to offer one version, in modesty, of how his thought might be logically extended into our own time.

While Maimonides ascribes a number of purposes to government, each of these, I believe, can be achieved within a liberal democratic framework. Political order in general for Maimonides is needed because of an inherent tension in human sociability: On the one hand, we are not Robinson Crusoes; we need society to fulfill our needs.[237] On the other hand, our natural differences generate friction and antagonism. A principal function of law, therefore, is to render these differences irrelevant by unifying our conventions: It "corrects" deficient human actions; "reins in" excessive ones; "ordains" others; and "fosters strains of character" toward the end of forming a "well ordered community" characterized by a "common and consistent ethos."[238] Liberals have historically held diverse views about our social tendencies. Still, Maimonides' empirical account strongly anticipates one of the most prominent, Immanuel Kant's "unsocial sociability:" While we cannot but exist in society with others, our proximity generates jealousy, antagonism, and domination, justifying the need for coercive juridical order.[239]

---

[236] In so far as Maimonides would know a concept of "democracy," it would likely be the one described by Plato and al-Fārābī, which for the latter is actually a kind of anarchy – a government by the unchecked and unchanneled passions of the populace: "If their situation is examined closely, it turns out that in truth there is no ruler among them and no ruled." *Political Regime*, 86. See Plato, *Republic*, 557a–58c.

[237] *Guide*, 1:72.

[238] *Guide*, 2:40. Maimonides also discusses our natural differences in *Mishneh Torah, Hilchot De'ot [Human Dispositions]*, 1:1.

[239] See especially the fourth "Proposition" in his "Idea for a Universal History with a Cosmopolitan Purpose," in *Kant: Political Writings*, ed. H. S. Reiss (Cambridge: Cambridge University Press, [1784] 2008). For an extended discussion of how this concept fits into Kant's larger ethical and political project, as well as liberalism more generally, see my *Solidarity in a Secular Age*, chapter 2.

What about the normative functions of government? Maimonides ascribes to the Torah two broad aims: "spiritual well-being," referring to how we learn truths about the world, either in the form of real knowledge or true beliefs; and "material well-being," referring to how we form a society grounded in legal justice ("quelling wrongdoing") and moral virtue ("acquiring traits of character beneficial to society and conducive to the civic order"). While both are important, the former is "higher and weightier" – the Torah's true end – while the latter is merely a means.[240] In one sense, then, what Maimonides prescribes takes him far from liberalism. The idea that a state should direct its citizens' moral and intellectual development reflects exactly the kind of infantilizing stance that liberal theorists from Kant to J.S. Mill, John Rawls, and Judith Shklar rejected so vehemently.[241]

Yet upon closer inspection, this gap narrows or even disappears. The critical distinction again is between ends and means, *telos* and *technē*. To begin with, liberal states also provide for legal order and social stability. To invoke Maimonides' own example, they are ones in which frail money changers need not fear hulking brutes.[242] More deeply, while liberals have historically rejected the state as an *instrument* for inculcating virtue, many have not abandoned the *end* of realizing ethical life and solidarity. Communitarians and nationalists often charge liberals with splitting us into social atoms. Yet as Bryan Garsten has recently argued, liberalism is best understood as a modification of rule – an attenuation of concentrated power – not a "self-sufficient way of life, philosophy or ideology . . . meant to stand on its own." Indeed liberals, contrary to caricature, most often assume the opposite of a "possessive individualism": Human beings will naturally form communities within which they will cultivate moral personality (including Jewish religious communities regulated by *halacha*).[243] In Maimonides' terms, they will

---

[240] Nonetheless, justice and virtue remain necessary prerequisites of intellectual development. See *Guide*, 3:27. In Maimonides' summary, each command in the Torah has one of three aims: "Imparting a belief, instilling a virtue, or curbing wrongdoing." *Guide*, 3:28. See also 3:31.

[241] As Shklar writes, for example, in discussing Kant, "Despotism reduced its subjects to perpetual infancy, and that meant that they could not choose their characters at all. They would remain obedient children – and thoroughly nasty ones at that. Liberal government for bad characters did not promise us that freedom would make us good; it merely argued that it would remove the most horrible obstacles to any ethical undertaking that we might conceivably try." *Ordinary Vices* (Cambridge, MA: Harvard University Press, 1984), 235–36.

[242] "If someone asked you, say, 'Has this land a ruler?' you might reply, 'Certainly.' The evidence? You could say: 'You see this money changer, this frail little man with that great pile of dinars before him, and that hulking fellow standing there, gaunt and poor, begging for so much as a carob seed, and the money changer not only refuses but drives him off with a torrent of words. If not for fear of the ruler, the poor beggar would hardly stick at killing him or shoving him aside and taking the money. That proves this city has a ruler!'" *Guide*, 1:46. While Maimonides offers this parable in the context of asking how we can acquire knowledge of God (the ruler here is analogized to the deity), it implies features of his political thought as well.

[243] Bryan Garsten, "The Liberalism of Refuge." *Journal of Democracy*, vol. 35, no. 2, April 2024, pp. 136–51.

"foster strains of character." And while the virtues they acquire will come not from the state but civil society, the result they achieve will be the same. As Alexis de Tocqueville famously argued, within such associations "[s]entiments and ideas renew themselves, the heart is enlarged, and the human mind is developed."[244]

This has been among the Enlightenment's great discoveries: With the right structures and institutions, ethical and intellectual life can emerge spontaneously. A heavy-handed state is not only unnecessary but counterproductive. Counterintuitively, societies can achieve greater moral and rational development from organic pluralism than coerced uniformity. Maimonides could never have anticipated this development. His ideas can accommodate it. Indeed while Maimonides sometimes describes Torah law as propelling our progress in virtue and wisdom, elsewhere he quietly elides this intermediate step: "Our highest human attainment is fulfillment as a rational being, to have a mind that actually thinks and knows all that a human being can know about everything we can know. . . . Only once bodily wellbeing is secured can one reach that doubtless higher level of perfection."[245]

A seemingly higher obstacle is Maimonides' messianism; yet here too, it is possible to envision a reconciliation with liberal democracy. As we have seen, Maimonides' messiah is a human king, and in this capacity he is assigned a definitive role in realizing the messianic age. At the same time, a careful study of Maimonides' words suggest additional room for maneuver. Maimonides legally mandates monarchy. But he consistently describes the king's functions in instrumental terms. While a king may raise taxes, levy soldiers, and conquer lands, he may only do so to "promote the true religion, fill the world with righteousness, break the arm of the wicked, and fight God's war." He must act "for the sake of Heaven" – an echo of the passage from *Avot* with which Maimonides opens the *Guide* and which, as we have seen, he associates with divine rule.[246] Thus if, as Maimonides stresses, "we do not, a priori, appoint a king except to execute justice and fight wars," it is unclear, at least logically, why government must be monarchial. These functions can be performed by democratic states too.[247]

---

[244] Alexis de Tocqueville, *Democracy in America*, trans. Harvey C. Mansfield and Delba Winthrop (The University of Chicago Press, [1835–40] 2000), II 2.5. For more on civil society's place in contemporary liberal democracies, see my and Nancy L. Rosenblum's chapter "Civil Society and Government," in *The Oxford Handbook of Civil Society*, ed. Michael Edwards (New York: Oxford University Press, 2011).

[245] While Maimonides does conclude the passage by arguing that the "Torah of Moses our Teacher . . . came just to better us in both ways," he tellingly does not imply that we can summit the intellect *only* via the Torah's envisioned political order. *Guide*, 3:27.

[246] Forms of political power which do not extend divine rule, by contrast, are associated with idolatry: "Their aim, like that of the heathen kings, being to advance their own glory and interests but not to promote the glory of God." *Hilchot Teshuva*, 3:13.

[247] *Hilchot Melachim*, 4:10.

The same point can be applied to Maimonides' account of the messianic advent. Maimonides follows traditional sources in documenting the messiah's attributes and actions: He is a king of the Davidic line, learned in Torah, and teaches its precepts to others; he defeats Israel's enemies, rebuilds the Temple, and gathers in the exiles.[248] In describing the fully developed age itself, however, the messiah himself quietly falls away. His role and rule cease to be relevant. What we find instead is a world in which politics has run its teleological course toward disseminating and elevating knowledge of God:

> At that time there will be no famines and no wars, no envy and no competition. For the Good will be very pervasive. ... The world will only be engaged in knowing God. Then, there will be very wise people who will understand the deep, sealed matters. They will then achieve knowledge of the Creator to as high a degree as humanly possible, as it says, *"For the Earth shall be filled with knowledge of the Lord, as the waters cover the sea."* (Isaiah 11:9)[249]

Here is nothing less than divine rule manifest on earth. Political order creates the conditions for cultivating moral virtue, which in turn allows for the diligent pursuit of wisdom. We achieve individual providence through our intellectual elevation. We model our actions on God's "goodness." And insofar as we know and imitate Him, God can be said to rule. The messianic age, in other words, is Maimonidean theocracy in completed form.

This is undoubtedly a utopian image; is it one whose realization depends on the particularities of Maimonides' political program? One element which might be necessary is national independence. In the *Guide*, Maimonides links Israel's loss of prophecy to its exile: Summitting the intellect requires intense self-development in discipline, virtue, and knowledge, and this is hardly feasible, on a national level, in the "infinite danger" of statelessness.[250] The messiah himself, however, seems to be a figure of provisional rather than intrinsic significance. Twice in the *Mishneh Torah* Maimonides invokes a well-known dictum from the rabbinic sages which, in effect, broadens the possible pathways

---

[248] *Hilchot Melachim*, 11:4.   [249] *Hilchot Melachim*, 12:5.

[250] The quote on statelessness is from Michael Walzer, *Spheres of Justice: A Defense of Pluralism and Equality* (New York: Basic Books, 1983), 34; *Guide*, 2:36. This may be one reason why Maimonides, when describing the rationale for Channukah festival, opens with the Hasmonean's military victory over the Greeks: It restored Jewish sovereignty to the land of Israel. Indeed Maimonides notes only in passing, and without negative comment, that the Hasmoneans made kings from priests in violation of *halacha*: "[The Hasmoneans] set up a king from among the priests and Israel's kingdom was restored for a period of more than two centuries." *Hilchot Megillah v'Chanukah [Scroll of Esther and Chanukah]*, 3:1. Maimonides here notably diverges from the Talmudic sages, who – likely because of the Hasmonean dynasty's many *halachic* improprieties – explained the holiday only in terms of the miracle of the oil. See Talmud Bavli, Tractate Shabbat, 21b.

toward the messianic age and deemphasizes its preconditions: "The only difference between the present and the Messianic era is that political oppression will
then cease."[251] It is hard to imagine hunger, violence, and social pathology
finally disappearing. It is equally difficult to envision people devoting all their
energies to wisdom and *imitatio dei*. A messianic king could conceivably bring
about each of these outcomes. But this is an article of faith and an inheritance of
tradition, not an inference of reason. In short: Monarchy, for Maimonides, might
be a *halachic* requirement of Jewish messianism. In his teleological account,
however, it is not a *practical* one.

There is a well-known moral concern about Maimonides' teleology: If the
real point is to know God, why do we still have to be good? Or grant that we
need moral virtue to climb philosophy's ladder; having reached the top, can't we
just kick it away? Lenn Goodman, connecting his own theory of justice to
Jewish sources, describes Maimonides' answer as the "virtuous circle" of the
messianic age.[252] Our intellectual objective is to know God. But as we have
seen, knowledge of God inspires not withdrawal from the world, but love of it. It
stirs us to emulate divine goodness. As we practice justice (*mishpat*), righteousness (*tzedakah*), and kindness (*chesed*), we come to see these very qualities
reflected in the cosmological design. Our greater wisdom then deepens our love,
taking us back around the circle. In Maimonides' words, "according to the
knowledge, will be the love."[253]

Our final question, therefore, is this: Under what conditions will we pursue
knowledge of God? What will make us more likely to love Him? Maimonides
does admit the practical need, historically, for threats of punishment and
promises of reward. As he writes in his tractate on "Repentance" [*Hilchot
Teshuva*], only the rare individual "does what is true because it is true."
Nonetheless, all should strive for something higher: to serve God out of love,
the "standard which God, through Moses, bid us to achieve."[254] Advocates for
a *halachic* state believe legal enforcement is necessary for theocracy. If the law

---

[251] *Hilchot Teshuva*, 9:2; *Hilchot Melachim*, 12:2.

[252] Lenn E. Goodman, *On Justice: An Essay in Jewish Philosophy* (New Haven: Yale University Press, 1991), ch. 5.

[253] *Hilchot Teshuva*, 10:6.

[254] *Hilchot Teshuva*, 10:2. Maimonides elsewhere compares the way we make progress in our moral motivation to the way a teacher instills love of learning in a pupil: As children, we are promised candies and trinkets for our studies; as adolescents, we learn to outdo our peers in honor; finally, in adulthood we pursue ideas out of a love of truth. Again anticipating Kant, Maimonides describes this process as a kind of *bildung*: "Our Sages knew how difficult a thing this [serving God out of pure love] was and that not everyone could act up to it. . . . Therefore, in order that the common folk might be established in their convictions, the Sages permitted them to perform meritorious actions with the hope of reward, and to avoid the doing of evil out of fear of punishment . . . until eventually the intelligent among them come to comprehend and know what truth is and what is the most perfect mode of conduct." *Introduction to Chelek*.

itself is the point, then only when the law is obeyed will God truly be crowned as sovereign. Maimonides' ideas, I have tried to show, take us in a different direction. In today's open societies, science, philosophy, and theology – our pathways, for Maimonides, to divine wisdom – are not the possession of a cloistered elite; they circulate in public reason.[255] Religious coercion might have contributed to social order in the past. But in a post-Enlightenment age, it would lead to neither knowledge nor love of God. Imposing *halacha* would pour water on the pursuit of wisdom and smother the sparks of affection. It would transform our actions into products of fear, conditioning, and servitude. Far from bringing about divine rule, it would turn God into a tyrant.

Maimonides, as evidenced by his discussion of sacrifices, believes in humanity's intellectual progress. Perhaps he would accept this account of our moral progress too: Rather than a theocracy in which *halacha* is forced upon us, we should seek one in which human beings freely choose, from their growing knowledge of the world, to voluntarily love and emulate the divine being; a theocracy where the true hallmarks of God's sovereignty – justice, righteousness, and kindness – are nurtured by liberal guarantees of stability, equality, and freedom for all; a theocracy set not in opposition to democracy, but alongside it. Whether God rules in heaven is assured. Whether He does here – whether the Good does here – is in our hands.

---

[255] Maimonides held by the Neoplatonic cosmology of his period because it was considered the cutting edge of science and philosophy. He also recognized that human knowledge makes progress, observing, for example, that mathematics and astronomy have advanced since Aristotle. *Guide*, 2:4, 3:14. It is impossible to know how he would have responded to the intellectual developments since his time. Neoplatonism's collapse does seem to render elements of his thought less tenable. Still, genuine philosophers are committed to truth, not dogma (see note 127). And Maimonides' broader concept – that knowledge of the world brings us toward knowledge of God – remains as applicable as ever. Insofar as we take direction from his thought, therefore, humanity's intellectual advances can only be seen in a positive light.

Bibliography

1 Samuel.

Adamson, Peter. *The Arabic Plotinus*. London: Duckworth, 2002.

al-Farabi. "The Attainment of Happiness." Translated by Muhsin Mahdi. In *Medieval Political Philosophy: A Sourcebook*, edited by Ralph Lerner and Muhsin Mahdi. New York: Free Press of Glencoe, 1963, pp. 58–82.

"Book of Religion." Translated by Charles E. Butterworth. In *The Political Writings: "Selected Aphorisms" and Other Texts*, edited by Charles E. Butterworth. Ithaca: Cornell University Press, 2015, pp. 85–114.

"The Harmonization of the Two Opinions of the Two Sages: Plato the Divine and Aristotle." Translated by Charles E. Butterworth. In *The Political Writings: "Selected Aphorisms" and Other Texts*, edited by Charles E. Butterworth. Ithaca: Cornell University Press, 2015, pp. 115–68.

"On the Intellect." Translated by Jon McGinnis and David C. Reisman. In *Classical Arabic Philosophy: An Anthology of Sources*, edited by Jon McGinnis and David C. Reisman. Indianapolis: Hackett, 2007, pp. 68–77.

"The Philosophy of Aristotle." Translated by Muhsin Mahdi. In *Alfarabi's Philosophy of Plato and Aristotle*, edited by Muhsin Mahdi. New York: The Free Press of Glencoe, 1962, pp. 71–132.

"The Philosophy of Plato." Translated by Muhsin Mahdi. In *Alfarabi's Philosophy of Plato and Aristotle*, edited by Muhsin Mahdi. New York: Free Press of Glencoe, 1962, pp. 53–70.

"Political Regime." Translated by Charles E. Butterworth. In *The Political Writings: "Political Regime" and "Summary of Plato's Laws,"* edited by Charles E. Butterworth. Ithaca: Cornell University Press, 2015, pp. 3–96.

"Selected Aphorisms." Translated by Charles E. Butterworth. In *The Political Writings: 'Selected Aphorisms' and Other Texts*, edited by Charles E. Butterworth. Ithaca: Cornell University Press, 2015, pp. 1–68.

Albeck, Hanoch. *Mavo La-Mishnah [Introduction to the Mishnah]*. Jerusalem: Bialik Institute, 1967.

Altmann, Alexander. "Maimonides' Four Perfections." *Israel Oriental Studies* 2 (1972): pp. 23–34.

Asad, Talal. *Formations of the Secular: Christianity, Islam, Modernity*. Stanford: Stanford University Press, 2003.

Belfer, Ella. *Am Yisrael U-Malkhut Shamayim [The People of Israel and the Kingdom of Heaven]*. Ramat-Gan: Bar-Ilan, 1980.

Berger, Peter, ed. *The Desecularization of the World: Resurgent Religion and World Politics*. Grand Rapids: William B. Eerdmans, 1999.

The Sacred Canopy. Garden City: Anchor Books, 1969.

Berman, Lawrence V. "The Political Interpretation of the Maxim: The Purpose of Philosophy Is the Imitation of God." *Studia Islamica* 15 (1961): pp. 55–61.

"Maimonides on Political Leadership." In *Kinship and Consent: The Jewish Political Tradition and Its Contemporary Uses*, edited by Daniel Elazar. Philadelphia: Turtledove, 1981, pp. 113–25.

"Maimonides, the Disciple of Alfarabi." *Israel Oriental Studies* 4 (1974): pp. 154–78.

Blidstein, Gerald. `Ekronot Mediniyim Be-Mishnat Ha-Rambam [Political Concepts in Maimonidean Jurisprudence]*. Ramat-Gan: Bar-Ilan, 1983.

Bloom, Pazit Ben-Nun and Gizem Arikan. "Democratic Norms and Religion." In *The Oxford Encyclopedia of Politics and Religion*, edited by Mark J. Rozell, Paul A. Djupe, and Ted G. Jelen. New York: Oxford University Press, 2020, pp. 241–61.

Blumenberg, Hans. *The Legitimacy of the Modern Age*. Translated by Robert M. Wallace. Cambridge, MA: MIT Press, [1966] 1983.

Butterworth, Charles E. "Alfarabi's Goal: Political Philosophy, Not Political Theology." In *Islam, the State, and Political Authority: Medieval Issues and Modern Concerns*, edited by Asma Afsaruddin. New York: Palgrave-MacMillan, 2011, pp. 53–74.

Calhoun, Craig, Mark Juergensmeyer and Jonathan VanAntwerpen, ed. *Rethinking Secularism*. New York: Oxford University Press, 2011.

Casanova, José. *Public Religions in the Modern World*. Chicago: The University of Chicago Press, 1994.

Cohen, Hermann. *Ethics of Maimonides*. Translated by Almut Sh. Bruckstein. Madison: University of Wisconsin Press, [1908] 2004.

Cooper, Julie. *Secular Powers: Humility in Modern Political Thought*. Chicago: The University of Chicago Press, 2013.

Davidson, Herbert Alan. "Maimonides' Shemonah Peraqim and Alfarabi's Fusul Al-Madani." *Proceedings of the American Academy of Jewish Research* 31 (1963): pp. 33–50.

Moses Maimonides. Oxford: Oxford University Press, 2005.

"Maimonides' Secret Position on Creation." In *Studies in Medieval Jewish History and Literature*, edited by Isadore Twersky. Cambridge, MA: Harvard University Press, 1979, pp. 16–40.

Faur, José. *The Horizontal Society: Understanding the Covenant and Alphabetic Judaism*. 2 Vols. Boston: Academic Studies Press, 2009.

Feinstein, Moshe. *Responsa of Rav Moshe Feinstein*. Translated by Moshe David Tendler. Vol. 1, Hoboken: Ktav, 1996.

Forte, Doron. "Back to the Sources: Alternative Versions of Maimonides' Letter to Samuel Ibn Tibbon and Their Neglected Significance." *Jewish Studies Quarterly* 23 (2016): pp. 47–90.

Foucault, Michel. *Security, Territory, Population*. Translated by Graham Burchell. Edited by Michel Senellart. New York: Picador, 1978.

Fraenkel, Carlos. *Philosophical Religions from Plato to Spinoza*. New York: Cambridge University Press, 2012.

ed. *Traditions of Maimonideanism*. Boston: Brill, 2009.

Funkenstein, Amos. *Nature, History, and Messianism in Maimonides [Hebrew]*. Tel Aviv: Misrad Ha-Bitachon, 1983.

Galston, Miriam. "Philosopher-King vs. Prophet." *Israel Oriental Studies* 88 (1978): pp. 204–18.

Politics and Excellence: The Political Philosophy of Alfarabi. Princeton: Princeton University Press, 1990.

Garsten, Bryan. "The Liberalism of Refuge." *Journal of Democracy*, 35, no. 2, (April 2024): pp. 136–51.

Gauchet, Marcel. *The Disenchantment of the World: A Political History of Religion*. Translated by Oscar Burge. Princeton: Princeton University Press, [1985] 1997.

Gerson, Lloyd. *From Plato to Platonism*. Ithaca: Cornell University Press, 2013.

Gillespie, Michael Allen. *The Theological Origins of Modernity*. Chicago: The University of Chicago Press, 2008.

Goodman, Lenn E. *A Guide to the* Guide to the Perplexed*: A Reader's Companion to Maimonides' Masterwork*. Stanford: Stanford University Press, 2024.

The Holy One of Israel. Oxford: Oxford University Press, 2019.

Love Thy Neighbor as Thyself. New York: Oxford University Press, 2008.

"Maimonides' Philosophy of Law." *Jewish Law Annual* 1 (1978): pp. 72–107.

On Justice: An Essay in Jewish Philosophy. New Haven: Yale University Press, 1991.

Gordon, Peter E. "The Erotics of Negative Theology: Maimonides on Apprehension." *Jewish Studies Quarterly* 2 (1995): pp. 1–38.

Gutas, Dimitri. "The Study of Arabic Philosophy in the Twentieth Century." *British Journal of Middle Eastern Studies* 29 (2002): pp. 19–25.

Guttmann, J. J. *Dat U-Madda [Science and Religion]*. Jerusalem: Magnes Press, 1955.

Habermas, Jürgen. "'The Political': The Rational Meaning of a Questionable Inheritance of Political Theology." In *The Power of Religion in the Public*

Sphere, edited by Eduardo Mendieta and Jonathan VanAntwerpen. New York: Columbia University Press, 2011, pp. 15–33.

Halbertal, Moshe. *Maimonides: Life and Thought*. Translated by Joel Linsider. Princeton: Princeton University Press, [2009] 2014.

People of the Book: Canon, Meaning, and Authority. Cambridge, MA: Harvard University Press, 1997.

Harris, Jay, ed. *Maimonides after 800 Years: Essays on Maimonides and His Influence*. Cambridge, MA: Harvard University Press, 2007.

Harvey, W. Zev. "Bein Filosofiyah Medinit Le-Halakhah Be-Mishnat Ha-Rambam [between Political Philosophy and Halakhah in Maimonides' Teachings]." *Iyyun* 29 (1980): pp. 198–212.

Harvey, Stephen. "Maimonides in the Sultan's Palace." In *Perspectives on Maimonides*, edited by Joel L. Kraemer. New York: Oxford University Press, 1991, pp. 33–46.

"The Place of the Philosopher in the City According to Ibn Bajja." In *Political Aspects of Islamic Philosophy*, edited by Charles E. Butterworth. Cambridge, MA: Harvard University Press, 1992, pp. 199–233.

Hirschl, Ran. *Constitutional Theocracy*. Cambridge, MA: Harvard University Press, 2010.

Hobbes, Thomas. *On the Citizen (De Cive)*. Edited and translated by Richard Tuck and Michael Silverthorne. Cambridge: Cambridge University Press, [1642] 2003.

Isaiah.

Ivry, Alfred. "Islamic and Greek Influence on Maimonides' Philosophy." In *Maimonides and Philosophy*, edited by Shlomo Pines and Yirmiyahu Yovel. Dordrecht: Martinus Nijhoff, 1986, pp. 139–56.

Kant, Immanuel. "Idea for a Universal History with a Cosmopolitan Purpose." In *Kant: Political Writings*, edited by H. S. Reiss. Cambridge: Cambridge University Press, [1784] 2008, pp. 41–53.

Kaye, Alexander. *The Invention of Jewish Theocracy: The Struggle for Legal Authority in Modern Israel*. New York: Oxford University Press, 2020.

Kellner, Menachem. *Dogma in Medieval Jewish Thought*. New York: Oxford University Press, 2004.

Maimonides on Human Perfection. Atlanta: Scholars Press, 1990.

Reinventing Maimonides in Contemporary Jewish Thought. New York: Oxford University Press, 2021.

Kraemer, Joel L. "Alfarabi's Opinions of the Virtuous City and Maimonides' Foundations of the Law." In *Studia Orientalia Memoriae D. H. Baneth Dedicata*, edited by Joshua Blau. Jerusalem: Magnes Press, 1979, pp. 107–53.

Maimonides: The Life and World of One of Civilization's Greatest Minds.
New York: Doubleday Religious Publishing Group, 2008.

Kreisel, Howard. *Maimonides' Political Thought: Studies in Ethics, Law, and
the Human Ideal*. Albany: SUNY Press, 1999.

Leibowitz, Yeshaiahu. *The Faith of Maimonides*. Translated by John Glucker.
New York: Adama, 1987.

Lerner, Ralph. *Maimonides' Empire of Light: Popular Enlightenment in an Age
of Belief*. Chicago: University of Chicago Press, 2000.

Lesch, Charles H. T. "Against Politics: Walter Benjamin on Justice, Judaism,
and the Possibility of Ethics." *American Political Science Review* 108, no.
1 (2014): pp. 218–32.

"Democratic Solidarity in a Secular Age? Habermas and the 'Linguistification
of the Sacred'." *The Journal of Politics* 81, no. 3 (2019): pp. 862–77.

"Radical Democracy's Religion: Hobbes on Language, Domination, and
Self-Creation." *Religions* 14, no. 11 (2023).

Solidarity in a Secular Age: From Political Theology to Jewish Philosophy.
New York: Oxford University Press, 2022.

"Theopolitics Contra Political Theology: Martin Buber's Biblical Critique of
Carl Schmitt." *American Political Science Review* 113, no. 1 (2019): pp.
195–208.

"What Undermines Solidarity? Four Approaches and Their Implications for
Contemporary Political Theory." *Critical Review of International Social
and Political Philosophy* 21, no. 5 (2018): pp. 601–15.

Lorberbaum, Menachem. *Politics and the Limits of Law: Secularizing the Political
in Medieval Jewish Thought*. Stanford: Stanford University Press, 2002.

Löwith, Karl. *Meaning in History: The Theological Implications of the Philosophy
of History*. Chicago: The University of Chicago Press, [1949] 1957.

Macy, Jeffrey. "Prophecy in Al-Farabi and Maimonides: The Imaginative and
Rational Faculties." In *Maimonides and Philosophy*, edited by
Shlomo Pines and Yirmiyahu Yovel. Dordrecht: Nijhoff, 1986,
pp. 185–201.

"A Study in Medieval Jewish and Arabic Political Philosophy: Maimonides'
Shemonah Peraqim and Al-Farabi's Fusul Al-Madani (or Fusul
Muntaza'ah)." Ph.D., The Hebrew University of Jerusalem, 1982.

Mahdi, Muhsin S. *Alfarabi and the Foundation of Islamic Political Philosophy*.
Chicago: University of Chicago Press, 2001.

Maimonides, Moses. "Epistle to Yemen." In *Epistles of Maimonides*, edited by
Abraham Halkin and David Hartman. Philadelphia: Jewish Publication
Society, 1985.

The Guide of the Perplexed, Volume 2. Translated by Shlomo Pines. Chicago: The University of Chicago Press, [1190] 1974.

The Guide to the Perplexed. Translated by Lenn E. Goodman and Phillip Lieberman. Stanford: Stanford University Press, [1190] 2024.

"Hakdama [Introduction]." In *Mishneh Torah*, edited by Zvi H. Preisler. Jerusalem: Ketuvim, [1180] 1993, pp. 1–3.

"Hilchot De'ot [Human Dispositions]." In *Mishneh Torah*, edited by Zvi H. Preisler. Jerusalem: Ketuvim, [1180] 1993, pp. 39–44.

"Hilchot Megillah V'chanukah [Scroll of Esther and Chanukah]." In *Mishneh Torah*, edited by Zvi H. Preisler. Jerusalem: Ketuvim, [1180] 1993, pp. 195–98.

"Hilchot Melachim U-Milhamoteihem [Kings and Their Wars]." In *Mishneh Torah*, edited by Zvi. H. Preisler. Jerusalem: Ketuvim, [1180] 1993, pp. 765–72.

"Hilchot Teshuva [Repentance]." In *Mishneh Torah*, edited by Zvi H. Preisler. Jerusalem: Ketuvim, [1180] 1993, pp. 59–66.

"Hilchot Yesodei Hatorah [Foundations of the Torah]." In *Mishneh Torah*, edited by Zvi H. Preisler. Jerusalem: Ketuvim, [1180] 1993.

"Introduction to Chelek." In *A Maimonides Reader*, edited by Isadore Twersky. New York: Behrman House, [1168] 1972, pp. 401–23.

Introduction to Pirkei Avot [Ethics of the Fathers]. Translated by Joseph I. Gorfinkle. [1168] 1966. www.sefaria.org.

Introduction to the Mishnah. Translated by Francis Nataf. [1168] 2017. www.sefaria.org.

Letters of Maimonides. Edited by Isaac Shailat. Jerusalem: Maaliyot Press, 1988.

"Mitzvot Aseh [Positive Commandments]." In *Mishneh Torah*, edited by Zvi H. Preisler. Jerusalem: Ketuvim, [1180] 1993.

"Mitzvot Lo Ta'aseh [Negative Commandments]." In *Mishneh Torah*, edited by Zvi H. Preisler. Jerusalem: Ketuvim, [1180] 1993.

Maimoun, Moïse ben. *Le Guide Des Égarés, Tome Premier*. Translated by Salomon Munk. Paris: A. Franck, [1190] 1856.

Meier, Heinrich, ed. *Gesammelte Schriften*. 3 Vols. Stuttgart: J. B. Metzler, 1996–2001.

Melamed, Abraham. *The Philosopher-King in Medieval and Renaissance Jewish Political Thought*. Albany: State University of New York Press, 2003.

Wisdom's Little Sister: Studies in Medieval and Renaissance Jewish Political Thought. Boston: Academic Studies Press, 2012.

Melzer, Arthur M. *Philosophy between the Lines: The Lost History of Esoteric Writing*. Chicago: University of Chicago Press, 2014.

Mishnah, Tractate Pirkei Avot.

Mittleman, Alan. "Theocratic Arguments in Judaism." In *Challenging Theocracy: Ancient Lessons for Global Politics*, edited by Toivo Koivukoski, David Edward Tabachnick, and Hermínio Meireles Teixeira. Toronto: University of Toronto Press, 2018, pp. 148–66.

Moyn, Samuel. *Christian Human Rights*. Philadelphia: University of Pennsylvania Press, 2015.

Namazi, Rasoul. *Leo Strauss and Islamic Political Thought*. New York: Cambridge University Press, 2022.

Nelson, Eric. *The Theology of Liberalism*. Cambridge, MA: Harvard University Press, 2019.

Orwin, Alexander. *Redefining the Muslim Community: Ethnicity, Religion, and Politics in the Thought of Alfarabi*. Philadelphia: University of Pennsylvania Press, 2017.

Parens, Joshua. *An Islamic Philosophy of Virtuous Religions: Introducing Alfarabi*. Albany: SUNY Press, 2006.

Leo Strauss and the Recovery of Medieval Political Philosophy. Rochester: University of Rochester Press, 2016.

Maimonides and Spinoza: Their Conflicting Views of Human Nature. Chicago: University of Chicago Press, 2012.

Metaphysics as Rhetoric: Alfarabi's Summary of Plato's Laws. Albany: SUNY Press, 1995.

Pines, Shlomo. "The Limitations of Human Knowledge According to Al-Farabi, Ibn Bajja, and Maimonides." In *Studies in Medieval Jewish History and Literature*, edited by Isadore Twersky. Cambridge, MA: Harvard University Press, 1979, pp. 1–82.

"The Philosophical Sources of the Guide of the Perplexed." Translated by Shlomo Pines. In *The Guide of the Perplexed*, edited by Shlomo Pines. Chicago: University of Chicago Press, 1963, pp. lvii–cxxxiv.

Plato. *Meno and Phaedo*. Translated by Alex Long. Edited by David Sedley. New York: Cambridge University Press, 2010.

Republic. Edited by Allan Bloom. New York: Basic Books, 1991.

Theaetetus and Sophist. Translated by Christopher Rowe. New York: Cambridge University Press, 2015.

Pollock, Benjamin. "'Every State Becomes a Theocracy': Hermann Cohen on the Israelites under Divine Rule." *Jewish Studies Quarterly* 25, no. 2 (2018): pp. 181–99.

Putnam, Robert D. *American Grace: How Religion Divides and Unites Us*. New York: Simon & Schuster, 2010.

Ravitzky, Aviezer. *Maimonides: Traditionalism, Originality, and Revolution.* Jerusalem: Merkaz Shazar Press, 2009.

"Philosophy and Leadership in Maimonides." In *Maimonides after 800 Years: Essays on Maimonides and His Influence,* edited by Jay M. Harris. Cambridge, MA: Harvard University Press, 2007, pp. 257–90.

Religion and State in Jewish Philosophy: Models of Unity, Division, and Subordination. Jerusalem: Israel Democracy Institute, 2002.

Rawls, John. "The Idea of Public Reason Revisited." *The University of Chicago Law Review* 64, no. 3 (1997): pp. 765–807.

Reale, Giovanni. *The Concept of First Philosophy and the Unity of the Metaphysics of Aristotle.* Translated by John R. Catan. Albany: SUNY Press, 1980.

Rosenblum, Nancy L. and Charles H. T. Lesch. "Civil Society and Government." In *The Oxford Handbook of Civil Society,* edited by Michael Edwards. New York: Oxford University Press, 2011, pp. 285–97.

Saiman, Chaim N. *Halakhah: The Rabbinic Idea of Law.* Princeton: Princeton University Press, 2018.

Schmitt, Carl. *Political Theology: Four Chapters on the Concept of Sovereignty.* Translated by George Schwab. Chicago: The University of Chicago Press, [1934] 2005.

Schwarzschild, Steven. "Moral Radicalism and 'Middlingness' in the Ethics of Maimonides." *Studies in Medieval Culture* 11 (1977): pp. 65–94.

Sedley, David. "Becoming Godlike." In *The Cambridge Companion to Ancient Ethics,* edited by Christopher Bobonich. New York: Cambridge University Press, 2017, pp. 319–37.

Seeskin, Kenneth, ed. *The Cambridge Companion to Maimonides.* Cambridge: Cambridge University Press, 2005.

Searching for a Distant God. New York: Oxford University Press, 2000.

Shapiro, Mark. *Studies in Maimonides and His Interpreters.* Scranton: University of Scranton Press, 2008.

Sharples, Robert. "Alexander of Aphrodisias on Divine Providence." *Classical Quarterly* 32 (1982): pp. 198–211.

Shklar, Judith. *Ordinary Vices.* Cambridge, MA: Harvard University Press, 1984.

Smith, Steven B. *Modernity and Its Discontents.* New Haven: Yale University Press, 2018.

Soloveitchik, Joseph B. *Maimonides: Between Philosophy and Halakhah.* Edited by Lawrence J. Kaplan. New York: KTAV, [1950–51] 2016.

Stern, Joseph. *Problems and Parables of Law: Maimonides and Nahmanides on Reasons for the Commandments (Ta'amei Ha-Mitzvot).* New York: State University of New York Press, 1988.

Strauss, Leo. *Persecution and the Art of Writing*. Chicago: University of Chicago Press, 1952.

　Philosophy and Law: Contributions to the Understanding of Maimonides and His Predecessors. Translated by Eve Adler. Albany: SUNY Press, [1935] 1995.

　"Some Remarks on the Political Science of Maimonides and Farabi." *Interpretation* 18, no. 1 ([1936] 1990): pp. 3–30.

Stroumsa, Sarah. *Andalus and Sefarad: On Philosophy and Its History in Islamic Spain*. Princeton: Princeton University Press, 2019.

　Maimonides in His World: Portrait of a Mediterranean Thinker. Princeton: Princeton University Press, 2009.

Talmud Bavli, Tractate Bava Batra.

Talmud Bavli, Tractate Berachot.

Talmud Bavli, Tractate Menachot.

Talmud Bavli, Tractate Sanhedrin.

Talmud Bavli, Tractate Shabbat.

Talmud Bavli, Tractate Ta'anit.

Tamer, Georges, ed. *The Trias of Maimonides*. New York: Walter de Gruyter, 2005.

Taylor, Charles. *A Secular Age*. Cambridge: Belknap of Harvard University Press, 2007.

Tocqueville, Alexis de. *Democracy in America*. Translated by Harvey C. Mansfield and Delba Winthrop. Chicago: The University of Chicago Press, [1835–40] 2000.

Vallat, Philippe. *Farabi Et L'école D'alexandrie*. Paris: Vrin, 2004.

Vatter, Miguel. *Divine Democracy: Political Theology after Carl Schmitt*. New York: Oxford University Press, 2021.

　Living Law: Jewish Political Theology from Hermann Cohen to Hannah Arendt. New York: Oxford University Press, 2021.

Walzer, Michael. *Spheres of Justice: A Defense of Pluralism and Equality*. New York: Basic Books, 1983.

Walzer, Michael, Menachem Lorberbaum, and Noam Zohar, ed. *The Jewish Political Tradition, Volume 1: Authority*. New Haven: Yale University Press, 2000.

Weber, Max. *Economy and Society*. Translated by Hans Gerth, Ephraim Fischoff, Ferdinand Kolegar, et al. Edited by Guenther Roth and Claus Wittich. Berkeley: University of California Press, [1922] 1978.

　"Science as a Vocation." In *From Max Weber: Essays in Sociology*, edited by H. H. Gerth and C. Wright Mills. New York: Oxford University Press, [1917] 1958, pp. 129–58.

Weiler, Gershon. *Jewish Theocracy*. Leiden: Brill, [1976] 1988.

Acknowledgments

"Exile yourself to a place of Torah," counsels the Mishnah in Pirkei Avot, "and don't say that the Torah will follow you, because it's your colleagues who will make it yours" (4:14). While I have been spared exile, I have been blessed with remarkable colleagues. It is because of them that this study came to be. Early in graduate school, Michael Sandel suggested that I attend a Maimonides seminar with Moshe Halbertal, then a visitor at Harvard Law School. The experience was transformative, giving me my first glimpse into the depths of Jewish philosophy. My dissertation led me in other directions; yet Maimonides always seemed to follow close behind. My first teaching position was at Vanderbilt, where two colleagues, Lenn Goodman and Phil Lieberman, were finishing a new translation of the *Guide to the Perplexed*. I can't say whether I should credit luck or providence (not in Maimonides' sense!). But this study would not have been possible without their monumental achievement. The beautiful translation, including hundreds of erudite and engaging footnotes, as well as Lenn's brilliant companion volume, *A Guide to the* Guide to the Perplexed, immerses the reader in Maimonides' philosophical context and shows how he remains indispensable today. I am privileged to have been among the first to learn from it.

Many other colleagues have contributed to this study. I am deeply grateful to Leigh Jenco for inviting me to write for this series on Comparative Political Theory, as well as to two anonymous reviewers from Cambridge University Press for their valuable insights. Jeff Macy closely read the entire manuscript twice, asking incisive questions and offering thoughtful comments. Cole Aronson provided constructive feedback about the book's language, argument, and structure. Parts of this book were presented at the 2022 American Political Science Association annual meeting and the 2023 Association for Jewish Studies annual conference. I would like to thank Michael Rosenthal for his comments, as well as the participants in those panels – Ronnie Beiner, Lenn Goodman, Sarah Greenberg, Mira Morgenstern, Andrew Rehfeld, Hava Tirosh-Samuelson, and Kenneth Seeskin – for their lively discussion. The Hebrew University of Jerusalem has been an ideal academic home, and I am especially grateful to Gidi Rahat and Avner De-Shalit for their support and guidance. My sincere gratitude also to the Golda Meir Fellowship Fund for its assistance.

I sometimes think that everything I write should come with a disclaimer: Whatever worthwhile thoughts are written herein should not be credited to me alone, but exist only because of hours of conversations with my wife, love, and partner Beth. It also helps that she embodies *chesed* in the sense Maimonides describes. So, consider this work disclaimed. I dedicate it to her. My parents, John Lesch and Paula Fass, deserve a similar proviso. Our discussions about Jewish thought and their comments on the entire manuscript are only the latest chapter in a dialogue about life and ideas stretching back to my earliest memories. Their unwavering love and support made me who I am today and continue to sustain me.

I thought about thanking my children, Yehuda, Reena, Izzy, and Tova. After all, they are the center of my world; I can imagine no greater gift than the privilege of raising and knowing them. Plus, they are a lot of fun. But they should really be thanking *me* for a summer filled with extra treats and trips to the arcade so Abba could get some work done. So, when you get old enough to read this, you're welcome.

Charles H. T. Lesch

To Beth

About the Author

Dr. Charles H. T. Lesch is Senior Lecturer in Political Science at the Hebrew University of Jerusalem and the author of *Solidarity in a Secular Age: From Political Theology to Jewish Philosophy* (Oxford University Press, 2022). A political theorist who focuses on the intersection of religion and democracy, his research grapples with questions in contemporary political theory and practice by drawing from the history of European political thought, modern and classical Jewish thought, religious studies, social theory, and literature. His work has also appeared in the *American Political Science Review, The Journal of Politics, Perspectives on Politics, Critical Review of International Social and Political Philosophy*, and *Religions*, among other journals.

Cambridge Elements ≡

Comparative Political Theory

Leigh K. Jenco

London School of Economics

Dr. Leigh K. Jenco is Professor of Political Theory at the London School of Economics and associate editor of the American Political Science Review. Her research focuses on how late imperial and modern Chinese thought can formulate and address questions of broad political concern, and thereby contribute to ongoing debates in political theory over democratic action, the politics of knowledge, and cultural imperialism. She has published widely across the disciplines of political science, philosophy, and intellectual history and is the author of Changing Referents: Learning Across Time and Space in China and the West (Oxford University Press, 2015) and Making the Political: Founding and Action in the Political Theory of Zhang Shizhao (Cambridge University Press, 2010). With colleagues at the universities of Zurich, Heidelberg, and Madrid, she manages a Humanities in the European Research Area grant for the collaborative research project "East Asian Uses of the European Past: Tracing Braided Chronotypes" (2016–2019).

About the Series

This series will encourage normative and conceptual reflection in and on a broad range of global political thought, in a format that enables both contextual depth and substantive insight into key dilemmas of political life. Responding to urgent concerns as well as analyzing long-standing issues, and reflecting the methodological breadth of this important and expanding field, the collection will invite engagements with texts and media from multiple languages, genres, and time periods. Elements in this series will demonstrate the viability and meaning of historically-marginalized bodies of thought for audiences beyond their place of origin, while maintaining attention to the rich particularity of diverse global reflections on politics.

Cambridge Elements ≡

Comparative Political Theory

Made in the USA
Monee, IL
07 July 2026

56552278R00046